Use It! Don't Lose It!

LANGUAGE

Daily Skills Practice

Grade 8

by Marjorie Frank

IncentivePublications

Thanks to Erin Linton
for her assistance in researching topics,
checking facts, and tracking down trivia.

Illustrated by Kathleen Bullock
Cover by Geoffrey Brittingham
Edited by Jill Norris
Copy-edited by Cary Grayson

ISBN 978-0-86530-653-0

5   6   7   8   9   10   09

Printed by Sheridan Books, Inc., Chelsea, Michigan • September 2009
www.incentivepublications.com

Don't let those language skills get lost or rusty!

As a teacher you work hard to teach language skills to your students. Your students work hard to master them. Do you worry that your students will forget the material as you move on to the next concept?

If so, here's a plan for you and your students—one that will keep those skills sharp.

Use It! Don't Lose It! provides daily language practice for all the basic skills. There are five language problems a day, every day for 36 weeks. The skills are correlated to national and state standards.

Students practice all the eighth grade skills, concepts, and processes in a spiraling sequence. The plan starts with the simplest level of eighth grade skills, progressing gradually to higher-level tasks, as it continually circles around and back to the the same skills at a little higher level, again and again. Each time a skill shows up, it has a new context—requiring students to dig into their memories, recall what they know, and apply it to another situation.

The Weekly Plan — Five Problems a Day for 36 Weeks

Monday – Thursday ....
- one vocabulary or other word skills item
- one spelling or mechanics item (capitalization, punctuation)
- one grammar or language usage item

Monday and **Wednesday** ....
- one reading item
- one literature item

Tuesday and **Thursday** ....
- one writing item
- one research/information skills item

Friday ....
- one longer reading comprehension passage with questions
- one writing task

Contents

How to Use Daily Skills Practice

To get started, reproduce each page, slice the Monday–Thursday lesson pages in half or prepare a transparency. The lessons can be used . . .

- **for independent practice**—Reproduce the lessons and let students work individually or in pairs to practice skills at the beginning or end of a language class.
- **for small group work**—Students can discuss and solve the problems together and agree on answers.
- **for the whole class review**—Make a transparency and work through the problems together as a class.

Helpful Hints for Getting Started

- Though students may work alone on the items, always find a way to review and discuss the answers together. In each review, ask students to describe how they solved the problem-solving problems or other problems that involve choices of strategies.

- Allow more time for the Friday lesson, as these tasks may take a little longer. Students can work in small groups to discover and discuss their answers.

- Provide dictionaries and other resources that may be helpful to students as needed. There will not always be room on the sheet for some of the longer writing tasks.

- Many of the writing tasks can be expanded into full writing lessons. When you have time to do so, extend the activity to work on all or various stages of the writing process. Find time for students to share and enjoy their written products.

- The daily lessons are designed to be completed in a short time period, so that they can be used along with your regular daily instruction. However, don't end the discussion until you are sure all students "get it," or at least until you know which ones don't get something and will need extra instruction. This will strengthen all the other work students do in language class.

- Keep a consistent focus on thinking skills for reading comprehension activities. Allow students to discuss their answers, particularly those that involve higher level thinking skills such as drawing conclusions, inferring, predicting, or evaluating.

- Find ways to strengthen the knowledge and use of new vocabulary words students learn in the daily practice. Keep a running list of these words. Use them in classroom discussions and activities. Find ways to share and show off knowledge of the words. Encourage students to include the new words in their writing.

- Take note of which items leave some or all of the students confused or uncertain. This will alert you to which skills need more instruction.

- The daily lessons may include some topics or skills your students have not yet learned. In these cases, students may skip items. Or, you might encourage them to consider how the problem could be solved. Or, you might use the occasion for a short lesson that would get them started on this skill.

1. Circle letters that should be capitalized.

national football league player walter payton ran more than 16,000 yards in his 13-year career with the chicago bears.

2. What literary term matches this definition?

a series of events related to the action of a story

_____

3. Circle the prefixes that mean **not.**

atypical   imperfect   nonsense   expel

inactive   disapprove   illegible   unfair

4. Which sentence is complete?

a. Although the World Cup tournament is held every four years.

b. Soccer is the most popular sport in the world.

c. The only soccer player allowed to handle the ball

5. Which statements are opinions?

a. A golf ball has more than 400 dimples.

b. Ice dancing is more pleasant to watch than ice hockey.

c. Racquetball is the most physically demanding racquet sport.

d. A football field is 100 yards long without the end zones.

e. A basketball player cannot score more than three points with any one successful basket attempt.

Do you get a kick out of football?

1. What part of speech is the word **fly**?

The crowd cheered when Gracie caught the fly ball.

_____

2. What is the most precise word for the sentence?

When Max, the team's best player, chose to skip the big game, his teammates were _____.

○ amused   ○ bothered   ○ irate

3. Number the words in alphabetical order.

___ **service**   ___ **score**   ___ **scoring**

___ **scoreboard**   ___ **serve**   ___ **scored**

4. Circle the words which are synonyms for **indignant.**

peeved   detached   autonomous

indecent   piqued   incensed

5. Add correct punctuation to the sentences. Circle words that should be capitalized.

when the new york yankees headed for california they flew out of the john f kennedy airport did they fly over the grand canyon or the rocky mountains on their way

I caught you on the fly.

1. Identify the rhyme pattern in the poem.

> Throw, throw, throw the ball
> Toward the catcher's mitt.
> Let the umpire make a call,
> And hope it's not a hit!

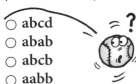

- ○ abcd
- ○ abab
- ○ abcb
- ○ aabb

2. Circle the correctly spelled words.

greif   reign   sleigh   conciet   beleive

3. What is the meaning of the bolded word?

I heard this game has been sold out for weeks, so how did you manage to **procure** seven tickets today?

4. Which sentences use **who** correctly?
a. To who should I give these tickets?
b. She's the one who bought the tickets.
c. Who is the player on third base?
d. For who are you saving this seat?

5. Circle the sentence that is out of sequence.

At the beginning of the second quarter, the Comets were behind by seven points. Abe scored six points in the third quarter to give the lead to the Comets. By half-time, the score was tied. The Grizzlies pulled ahead by eleven points in the fourth quarter.

1. Add the correct ending punctuation.

Watch out for that golf ball

2. An alphabetical list at the end of a book that helps locate information in the book is
- ○ a bibliography
- ○ a table of contents
- ○ an index
- ○ a preface

3. Circle the complete subject.

Jackie, wearing number ten, dribbled the ball all the way down the court.

4. What is the meaning of the word **morose**?

_____

_____

_____

5. Cross out the unnecessary words in this passage.

In my opinion, I think the game was a disaster. The two 16-year old teenage quarterbacks could share a prize for the worst, most awful plays of the night. I am sorry that I spent seven dollars for the ticket. I feel my money was wasted. Hopefully, I wish for a better game next week.

We did better at practice.

Read:

1. Identify the genre (type of writing) for each example.
2. What is the main idea in passage F?
3. Circle an example of hyperbole.
4. Which examples are expository?
5. What is the tennis coach's name?

It's love.

A. _____
Fifteen-year old Sam Garfus stunned a sold-out crowd at the state high school tennis championships yesterday. It was a surprise when the young player won straight sets to beat top-ranked players. The modest freshman explained that some lucky orange socks helped him win, but tennis pros around the state credit the victory to his outstanding skills.

B.
Sam: Why does Coach Stringer wear earplugs to every game?

Dan: Because he can't stand all the racket.

C. _____
The tennis matches started at 8 a.m. By 10 o'clock, the weather was so hot that the rubber was melting off the tennis balls, and the referee's nose had burst into flames twice. Nevertheless, Sam Garfus was playing his hottest game. Each time he hit a shot, he leaped 12 feet into the air and sent the ball above the clouds. In just under 45 seconds, he had won the tournament.

D.
In the game of tennis, two or four people play on a court that is divided by a low net. The players use racquets to hit a ball back and forth over the net. A point is scored when the ball bounces inside the boundaries of the court without being returned by another player.

E.
A young tennis player named Sam

Smacked ten balls, each time yelling, "Wham!"

_____

The crowd chanted his name

_____

F.
Dear Grandma,
Guess what? I won the state high school single's tennis championship yesterday! I am sure those orange socks helped me win. Thanks for knitting them for me. They were just as lucky as you said they would be.
Love ya,
    Sam

Write:

1. Write a headline for example A.
2. Write a title for example C.
3. Write the missing lines for the limerick E.

1. Circle the proper nouns.

Shamu	**Atlantic Ocean**	**sailor**
lifeguard	**Agate Beach**	**Bay Bridge**

2. Put commas where they are needed.

After swimming we picked up shells ate lunch put on sunscreen and napped on the beach.

3. Circle the compound words.

seaside	**submarine**	**undertow**
shipshape	**sandwich**	**waterlogged**
sunburn	**seaweed**	**underwater**

4. From this passage, can you tell how many circuli would indicate that a fish is three years old?

A fish's scales give a clue to its age. The scales have growth rings called circuli. These rings form in clusters called annuli. Each annulus (cluster) shows a year of age.

5. What can you tell about the bias of the person who wrote this sign?

NOTICE TO VISITORS
Visit this beach at your own risk.
The sand is scratchy and will get into your clothes and shoes.
The sun can burn you.
The wind can dry out your skin.
The water has slimy seaweed and you might smell dead fish.
Little children tend to be noisy and run around kicking up sand.

1. Which is the denotation of the word, **pirate**?
- ○ one who robs on seas or oceans
- ○ a dangerous person with an eye patch and a wooden leg who sails a black ship and steals gold

2. Circle the correctly spelled words.

raucous	**recklis**	**fearsome**
terrorize	**protectshun**	**explosion**
insurence	**despicible**	**dangereous**

3. Name five first person pronouns.

_____ _____ _____

_____ _____

4. The word **beachcomber** would be found on page _____.

5. Which are examples of persuasive writing?
- a. recipe for salmon-broccoli ice cream
- b. brochure advertising a fishing boat
- c. essay warning teenagers about tattoos
- d. tall tale about a boy who rode sharks
- e. directions to get to the lighthouse

bauble	**155**	bazaar
bazooka	**156**	beagle
beak	**157**	beard

1. Which is the simple sentence?

○ The Indian Ocean is the world's smallest, youngest, and most complex ocean.

○ It is 6,200 miles wide and covers a 28,000,000 square mile area.

○ The deepest point, off the southern coast of Java, is the Java Trench.

2. Circle the antonym for **malevolent**.

nefarious	**wholesome**
sullen	**furtive**

3. Capitalize the book title correctly.

twenty thousand leagues under the sea

4. Circle the cause. Draw a box around the effect.

Because the pirate ship sank in a wild storm, the treasure ended up at the bottom of the ocean.

5. What is the author's purpose for writing this?

STRANDED ON AN ISLAND SURROUNDED BY SHARKS. LEFT AUSTRALIA MARCH 5, 2004 HEADED FOR TAHITI. SHIP WRECKED AFTER 3 DAYS AT SEA. I CAN'T HOLD OUT MUCH LONGER.
IMA SUE LAHST
MARCH 22 (I THINK)

1. Give three different meanings of the word **charge**.

2. Correct the misspelled words.

lisence	**excape**
weird	**jeopardy**
cafateria	**whail**

3. Which sentence has correct pronoun use?

a. Whose yacht is next to the pirate ship?

b. Do you know who's run into the pier?

c. No, but I know who's life rafts are missing.

4. Rob is ready to write a paragraph that gives details about a ship, **The Maine Clipper**, that crashed into rocks during a storm on Halloween night. Write a topic sentence for this paragraph.

5. Examine the picture. Predict what will happen next.

Use It! Don't Lose It! IP 612-3

Read

1. What time must a visitor leave the beach on March 4?
2. What can you infer about the water temperatures?
3. What general conclusions can you draw about this area from reading all the signs?
4. Are picnics permitted on Red Rock Beach?

WELCOME TO
RED ROCK BEACH
ENJOY YOUR STAY

NO SWIMMING
OUTSIDE OF
AREAS
SUPERVISED BY
LIFEGUARD

Watch out!
Dangerous
Undertows

Wet Suits
Recommended
for Swimmers

Prohibited:
Dogs
Glass Containers
Alcohol
Surfing

WARNINGS
High Waves
Underwater Rocks

BEACH CLOSES
8 PM
Oct 1 - April 30
10 PM
May 1 - Sept 30

No Sleeping
Allowed on
Beach at Any
Time

Write

The structure of these sentences has confused the meaning.
Rewrite each sentence to clarify the meaning.

Squawk! I'm confused!

1. Mom whistled to her dog driving a dune buggy on Lost Creek Beach.
2. Alex and I laughed a lot when we had Sam for lunch on the beach.
3. Relaxing on my sailboat, a storm came in.
4. The blue swimmer's beach towel got washed away by a wave.
5. Lucy dropped into the ocean the new goggles she had bought by mistake.
6. Todd caught fish and served them to the girls seasoned with salt and pepper.
7. Paddling the raft to the shore, the picnic looked inviting.
8. While waiting on my surfboard, a jellyfish stung me.
9. Shakira saw a shark in her bathing suit ready to go into the water.
10. Tired and hot from running on the beach, the water looked good to us.

1. A story begins like this:

I have the honor of being the man with the world's longest beard. Let me tell you how I came to have this much hair on my chin.

What is the point of view?

_____

2. Does this sentence use an apostrophe correctly?

That girl's fingernails are long enough to set a record.

3. Which word means **to cause to feel terror**?

○ terrible   ○ terrify

○ terrific   ○ terrorism

4. Circle the correct word to complete the sentence.

Excited fans, eager to watch the marathon, (line, lines) up early to buy their tickets.

Do you get the point?

Imagine having the longest fingernails in the world! Lee Redmond, of the USA, has not cut her nails since 1979. The total length of all ten nails is 24 feet, 7.8 inches. She doesn't bite them; she won't sell them; and she only trims them occasionally. She claims they do not complicate her life much. It's safe to say, she is happy with this unusual characteristic.

5. Does the author have enough information to draw the conclusion written in the last sentence?

1. Rewrite the sentence to show more action.

With 13 balanced spoons, Jonathan Friedman is the world record-holder for balancing spoons on his face.

2. A record-holding juggler was showing off to his friends by juggling 20 kitchen utensils.

Was he **flaunting** or **flouting** his skills?

3. Which key word or phrase is best to use for an encyclopedia search for the world's longest tunnel?

tunnel   length   world

manmade   structures   longest

4. Correct the spelling of any misspelled words.

lafter   ghastly   chemist   jiant

gnome   riggle   shure   skwirt

5. Choose and circle the correct word for each sentence.

a. **(Anyway, Anyways)**, I can't believe you balanced all those spoons.

b. I found some broken plates **(beside, besides)** the juggler's van.

c. What's the difference **(between, among)** juggling balls or plates?

d. Who holds the record for **(setting, sitting)** in a tree the longest?

World Records

I'm going to have to read myself someday.

1. What is the meaning of this sentence?

While Kate has been doing that project, she has been burning the candle at both ends.

2. Insert the correct punctuation.

So my question is this Did you know that the longest tongue in the world measures 3.7 inches and belongs to Stephen Taylor (UK)?

3. Write a possessive phrase meaning **the peel of one banana**.

_____

4. To which sense does this description appeal most strongly?

The bubble-blowing championship was a melodious chorus of smacking and cracking, rhythmically swaying with whooshes and hisses, and pleasantly punctuated by regular pops!

5. Max got these books at the library. Examine the titles. What can you infer about Max's interests?

1. Correctly spell the plural of each word.

monkey   box   record

hoof   penny   pailful

2. Circle the word that does not belong.

waffle   heiress   pneumonia

gnome   knight   kneel

3. Circle the verbs that are in past tense.

swam   juggle   broke

argued   leapt   rise

4. Which reference source is a dictionary of geographical terms and places?

○ almanac   ○ periodical

○ atlas   ○ gazetteer

○ thesaurus   ○ quotation index

5. Write a caption for this picture of Tanya, the person with the longest hair in the state. Add any details or facts you wish to the description.

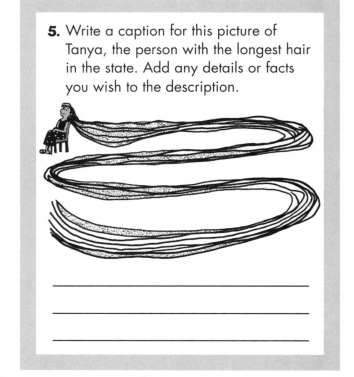

_____

_____

_____

12

Name

Read

1. How many of the records were set in the 20th century?

2. How many records were not set in North America?

3. If the snowball fighters joined the musical chair players, how large would the group be?

4. How many groups had fewer participants than the group hug?

5. Which event do you suppose took up the most space or distance?

It Takes A Group

Record	Date	Location	Number of Participants
Longest Human Chain	Aug 23, 1989	Eastern Europe	2,000,000
Largest Group Hug	Apr 23, 2004	Canada	5,117
Largest Circle Dance	May 6, 1995	UK	6,748
Largest Dog Walk	Jun 22, 2003	UK	4,372
Largest Snowball Fight	Jan 18, 2003	Switzerland	2,473
Largest Pajama-Sleepover Party	Feb 1, 2003	Virginia	1,045
Largest Game of Musical Chairs	Aug 5, 1989	Singapore	8,238
Longest Human Domino Line	Sept 30, 2000	Singapore	9,234

Conga!

Write

Think of yourself as a radio reporter covering one of the record-setting events above. Write a brief report that you will give, describing the event to your audience. Use your imagination to elaborate on what you think it might be like to watch the event.

WKRZ

1. Choose the correct literary device.

Huffing and puffing, the old locomotive complained grumpily as he trudged up the hill.

○ onomatopoeia   ○ irony

○ personification   ○ foreshadowing

2. Circle the objective pronouns.

We waited an hour for them at the train station and gave them a rousing welcome.

3. Write the past tense of each verb.

speed   **fight**   **read**

catch   **hurry**   **loosen**

4. Could an attempt to rob a train turn into a **debacle**? Explain.

Puff! Puff!

5. Write a summary of this story.

The Great Train Robbery of 1963 took place north of London. Robbers fixed the train signal to turn red and stop the train. Then 15 holdup men wearing masks, gloves, and helmets took 120 mailbags containing 2,600,000 British pounds. Two accomplices helped by providing train information and a hideout. There were no guns used in the robbery.

After the robbers left fingerprints at a hideaway, twelve of the robbers were caught and sent to prison. One robber, Ronnie Briggs, escaped from prison in 1965 and fled to Mexico. At age 71, he returned to Britain and was put in prison. The stolen money was never recovered.

1. Write the plural of each noun.

sister-in-law   **cactus**   **tooth**   **radio**

engineer   **watch**   **knife**   **mystery**

2. Which statement is true?

○ Fiction is organized alphabetically by titles.

○ Biographies are arranged alphabetically by the name of the author.

○ The Dewey Decimal System is used to organize nonfiction.

Curious.

3. Add correct punctuation to the sentence.

Officer, whispered the lady in the fur coat, that man's behavior is very suspicious.

4. What is the meaning of **surreptitious** in item 5?

5. Edit this passage for spelling, punctuation, and capitalization.

the strang man, on the trane plattform pulled his green hat down to sheeld his face And turned up the coller on his long baggy trench coat? he lingered in the shadows furtively sneeking out and darting back, to his hiding place behind a post, it wasn't long befor other passengers, began to notise his surreptitious behavour.

1. What is the main idea of this passage?

Bobbie Jo meant to rob the train. He had a mask and a gun. The mask was ripped off his face when it got caught on Mrs. Leevy's hat pin, and nobody was fooled by the squirt gun. When he stood up, intending to yell, "Get on the floor and empty your pockets," it came out like this: "Empty the floor and spit on your pockets!"

2. Circle the words that need capital letters.

dr. charles ryder bought pepsi cola before boarding the starlight express to portland, oregon.

3. What kind of sentence is this?

Give me all your money.

○ declarative   ○ imperative

○ exclamatory   ○ interrogative.

4. What is the tone of the passage in 1?

5. Replace each incorrect homonym.

TRAIN STATION RULES

Clothes the doors between compartments.

Have patients, do not bored the train until it stops.

By your tickets from the ticket cellar at the ticket window.

Bier or whine is not aloud on trains.

All violators will be cot and find.

1. A book about a person's life that is written by the subject of the book is a(n) _____

2. Circle the conjunction in this sentence.

When two high-speed trains pass each other, they must slow down so that their windows do not break.

3. Correct the spelling in these words.

celloes _____

potatoe_____

avacado _____

echoe _____

obo_____

saprano _____

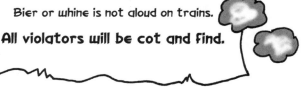

What's your timetable?

4. Finish the analogy

artisan : art :: traveler : _____

○ travel   ○ timetable   ○ train   ○ travelogue

5. Add a detail to the passage.

Before You Board The Train

The first thing you must remember when you are taking a train trip is to buy your ticket. Also, be sure that your suitcase is not too heavy to lift up the train steps. Take along some spending money to buy lunch on the train.

_____

_____

Above all, get to the train station on time!

Read

1. What is the purpose of the example?
2. If Mr. Smoots misses the 5:36 train out of Blythe headed for Newberry, where will he have to spend the night?
3. About how long is the Westbound trip between Silverton and Newberry?
4. Which two cities are probably closest together?
5. Where is the end of the westbound line?

GOLD COUNTY TRAIN SCHEDULE

Train A (Eastbound)

City:	Gulch	Jewel	Silverton	Vista	Blythe	Tomas	Newberry
arrival		7:33a	8:46a	10:30a	10:59a	11:14a	12:10a
departure	6:20a	7:36a	8:49a	10:35a	11:03a	11:19a	
arrival		10:22a	11:36a	1:37a	2:27p	11:44a	12:39a
departure	8:55a	10:25a	11:46a	1:45p	2:30p	2:47p	
arrival		2:10p	3:21p	5:00p	5:29p	6:50p	7:30p
departure	12:56p	2:13p	3:22p	5:05p	5:36p	6:55p	

Train B (Westbound)

City:	Newberry	Tomas	Blythe	Vista	Silverton	Jewel	Gulch
arrival		8:17a	8:46a	9:24a	10:16a	11:35a	12:46p
departure	7:15a	8:30a	8:50a	9:30a	10:20a	11:39a	
arrival		2:22p	2:37p	3:07p	3:50p	5:11p	6:20p
departure	1:20p	2:30p	2:40p	3:17p	3:55p	5:15p	
arrival		4:10p	4:28p	5:05p	5:57p	7:22p	8:35p
departure	3:15p	4:15p	4:35p	5:15p	6:01p	7:25p	

Write

Finish the comparisons.

1. A ride on a train is like _____.
2. That old steam engine sounds as _____ as _____.
3. The food on the train tasted like _____.
4. _____ is as loud as the train's whistle.
5. The bullet train is faster than _____.
6. The noise of the train on the rails reminds me of _____.
7. _____ is as thrilling as a ride on a high speed train.
8. The swaying of the train is like _____.

1. Circle examples with correct hyphen use.

roller-coaster   **one-half**

French-fries   **stomach-ache**

ex-president   **brother-in-law**

2. Which word does not belong?

○ exuberance   ○ ardor

○ enthusiasm   ○ exorbitance

3. Which is an example of imaginative writing?

a. a science fiction story about a 25th century amusement park

b. an article about the history of theme parks

c. a biography of the man who holds the world's record for time on a roller coaster

4. Fact or opinion?

Roller coasters are the most thrilling rides at any amusement park.

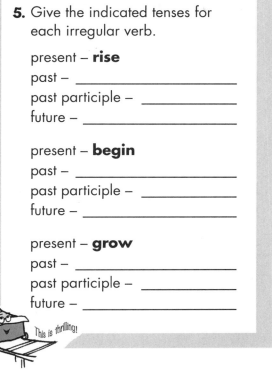
This is thrilling!

5. Give the indicated tenses for each irregular verb.

present – **rise**

past – _____

past participle – _____

future – _____

present – **begin**

past – _____

past participle – _____

future – _____

present – **grow**

past – _____

past participle – _____

future – _____

1. Michael recommends that Ralph avoid riding *The Terminator* roller coaster. Is Michael giving **advice** or **advise**?

Did you say thrilling?

2. Give the comparative and superlative forms of the adjective **thrilling**:

3. One word shows up twice in this sentence. Explain both meanings of the word.

Brie said, "I'll pass on the potatoes, but before long, she hollered, "Pass the fries!"

4. Cross out words in the sentence that are not needed to convey the meaning.

When we finish our rides, let's meet under that triangular sign that has three sides.

5. Tell three things you could learn from reading this encyclopedia entry.

Ferris Wheel, history

The first Ferris Wheel was designed by George Washington Gale Ferris. Thirty-six cars carried riders. Twelve different steel companies took part in the construction of the wheel, which cost $350,000. It towered 264 feet high, weighed 1,200 tons, and held 2,160 passengers at a time. The Ferris Wheel made its public debut at the World's Columbian Exposition in 1893. It proved to be a very popular ride.

1. What words or phrases create sensory appeal?

Waves of warm buttery popcorn-air wrapped around us and pulled us toward the popcorn stand.

2. Give an antonym for the word **plummet**.

_____

3. Choose the correct word for the sentence.

With their steep drops, these rides **(appeal, appeals)** to most teenage visitors at the theme park.

4. Correct the capitalization and punctuation in the heading of this letter.

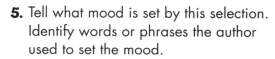

maria ruiz
335 court st
medford OR 97504

october 7 2005

5. The Scream Machine ride begins with a 200-foot fall followed by three hills and three steep dips and a screeching left hairpin turn. At the top of the fourth hill, the cars wind down a tight spiral track that leaves every rider with a spinning head. The ride finishes after nine more hills, twelve sharp curves, and nine dips.

On this ride, what happens just before the cars climb the fourth hill?

1. Use each of these words as a part of two compound words. Make it the beginning of one word and the ending of another.

light   book   over   board

2. Which example shows correct usage?
   a. To whom shall I give this cotton candy?
   b. Whom shall I say is calling?

Sweet!

3. Circle the correctly spelled words.

silliness   fancyful   worrysome

pennyless   terrifying   justified

4. Which information can be found in a dictionary?
   a. word histories   b. word meanings
   c. word pronunciations   d. synonyms

5. Tell what mood is set by this selection. Identify words or phrases the author used to set the mood.

Afraid she would miss the ride, Annie raced past the Haunted Village, dashed across the food court, and elbowed her way urgently through the crowded walkway. Just in time, she darted under the rope and tore around the side of the track. "Thanks for saving my place!" she panted as she scrambled into the front car of the roller coaster.

Read

1. Which selection is most convincing to you? Tell why.
2. Describe the main idea of each selection.
3. Describe the bias found in each selection.
4. Circle one fact in each selection.
5. Circle one opinion in each selection.
6. A rider in the back seat gets more airtime. Make an inference about the reason for this.

I'll take notes.

Take A Back Seat

The very best seat in a roller coaster is the last seat. As the coaster climbs each hill, you have the fun of watching each of the other cars disappear over the edge, and you get the longest time to anticipate the drop. Beyond that, this is the spot for the greatest speed. As that last car drops over the top, the roller coaster is going its fastest, and you get the tail end of that tremendous speed. In the back seat, you also get the longest airtime. This is the time that you fly up out of your seat, feeling weightless, because of inertia. And that's not all! You hear all of the screams along the ride, and the ride seems longer because your car pulls into the station last.

Go For The Front Seat

Run as fast as you can to get in the front seat of the roller coaster. This is the spot for the greatest thrills. Here, you will feel the greatest force of the wind as the coaster tears down the hills and around corners. It is only in the front that you can enjoy the unrestricted views and that amazing, terrifying feeling of being utterly alone at the steepest points of the ride. After the train of cars chug-chug-chugs to the top of the hill, only front riders get to feel that heart-stopping anticipation of dropping over the edge first. There is nothing ahead but empty space and the hope that there is, indeed, a track. No other seat in the coaster offers the same combination of dread and excitement.

Just write, it's just right.

Write

Write a short summary of one or both of the selections.

1. What is the meaning of the bolded word?

After 18 days on the trail, Teryl was getting hungry because of a **dearth** of food.

2. Which examples contain linking verbs?

a. Eric is a hiker on the Pacific Crest Trail.

b. By dinner time, he feels famished.

c. If he's lucky, he might cover 20 miles today.

3. Circle the correctly spelled words.

migrant	**accidant**	**negligent**
distant	**observent**	**vigilent**

4. What literary technique is used in this example?

A loud crash and a grinding crunch echoed from just around the bend on the trail. Lee stopped dead in his tracks. When ear-splitting cracks and snaps followed, he dropped his pack and sprinted in the opposite direction.

5. What kind of terrain is traveled by a thru-hiker on the Pacific Crest Trail?

Yo-de-lay-dee-hoo!

Eric Ryback is generally agreed to be the first person to thru-hike the Pacific Crest Trail. He carried an 80-pound pack as he completed the 2650-mile trail, which winds over mountain passes through canyons and forests, and crosses three states.

1 Is the punctuation correct?

The Pacific Crest Trail passes through: three national monuments; 24 national forests; 32 wilderness areas; and seven national parks.

2. Underline the indirect object.

The Pacific Crest Trail offers hikers a unique challenge.

3. Circle the correct word for the sentence.

Yesterday's hike was so long and hard; today, Simone was (**loath, loathe**) to get out of her tent.

4. Correct the punctuation and capitalization.

maomi vemura was the first man to reach the north pole alone this japanese explorer arrived at his goal on april 29 1978

Are you going in the right direction?

5.

adjust	25	admonish
admonition	26	advance
advantage	27	advise
adviser	28	affected

Write the dictionary page number on which each words would be found.

____ A. adventurous ____ D. aerial

____ B. ad-lib ____ E. admire

____ C. adorn ____ F. advertise

1. What is the meaning of this word's root?

vitality

_____ _____
     root   *meaning*

I keep a camper's journal.

DAY 6: FIND FOOD!

2. Circle the **effect** in this example.

Each time the hiker ran out of food, she was forced to forage something to eat from her natural surroundings.

3. Rewrite this sentence to show correct use of a negative.

Scarcely nobody has completed the Pacific Crest Trail yet this year.

4. Capitalize and punctuate the sentences correctly.

watch out for the falling rocks yelled Rod to the hiker behind him Samantha hollered back I see them

5. Identify one or more effective writing techniques used by the author.

An aggravated bear, fiercely roaring, bolted down the trail straight into the path of the hikers. They froze. Their hair stood on end. Bodies quivered. Muscles shivered. No one could move—no one but the bear, that is. Claws throwing up clods of earth, mighty weight smashing branches, breath steaming rhythmically like a well-fueled locomotive—the bear kept moving closer, closer.

1. Which means **freedom from punishment**?

  ○ indictment   ○ impunity

  ○ impertinence   ○ illicit

2. Write a word that contains a silent letter that fits each definition.

chocolate candy   apparition   pack animal

giggle   mute   pen name

3. What part of a book lists, in outline form, the information contained in the book in the order in which appears?

4. Circle the **preposition**. Draw a box around the **object of the preposition**.

Her blisters were so painful that Brooke could only hobble along the trail slowly.

5. Rewrite each sentence in active voice.

  A. Joe seemed miserable with his mosquito bites.

  B. That bear is really close!

  C. Tom is probably on the wrong trail.

  D. Does it appear to be thundering?

My blisters have blisters.

Use It! Don't Lose It! IP 612-3

Read

1. Could someone travel by water from Diamond Lake to Rainbow Campsite?

2. What bodies of water are crossed by Paradise Trail?

3. About how long is Last Chance Lake?

4. Which campsite is farthest from North Fork Creek?

5. What direction is Agate Butte from the ranger station?

Title: Paradise Valley Wilderness Area

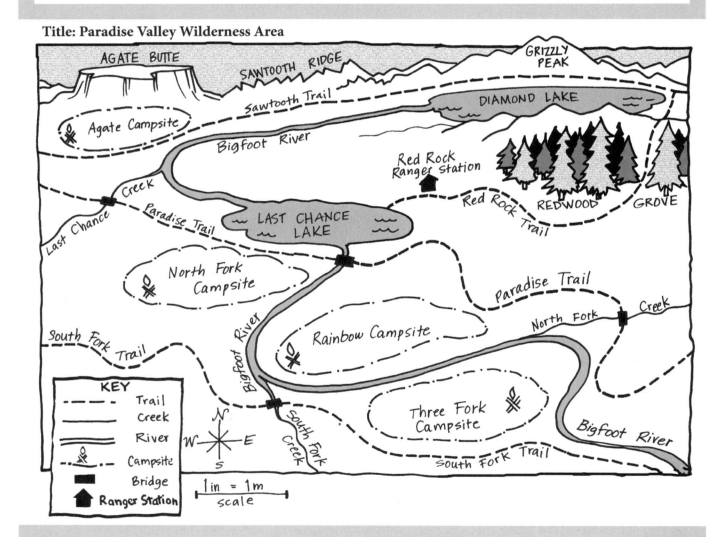

Write

Write clear directions that a hiker could follow to get from Three Fork Campsite to Agate Butte passing through Redwood Grove.

1. Write a homonym for each word.

fowl **carrot** **pour**

symbol **toad** **rap**

2. Correct the misspelled words.

When they went for a liesurely swim, niether Al nor Sal noticed the wierd creature floating along the shore.

3. Circle the correct pronoun.

Few divers were disappointed by the sights **(he, they)** saw.

4. A writer uses these words and phrases to set a certain mood in a passage. What is the mood?

drowsy eyelids _____

languid music _____

sluggish steps _____

meandering dreams _____

Glub
Glub

5. Identify two similarities of and two differences between free diving and scuba diving.

There are two basic kinds of underwater diving outside of a protective vehicle. Although both kinds of diving allow people to enjoy the wonders of life below the surface, they are quite different. The simplest and oldest form is called free diving. Divers use a mask, a snorkel, or possibly a wet suit. They must hold their breath and can only descend about 30 or 40 feet. They must come to the surface in a minute or two. Scuba diving is the second basic kind of diving. Scuba-diving equipment allows divers to go much deeper. The breathing apparatus supplies air so they do not have to hold their breath. The usual equipment includes a mask, tank, wet suit, hose, and regulator.

1. Explain the meaning of the sentence.

Even though the water was cold, I was sweating bullets as I got ready for my first deep sea dive.

2. Correct the capitalization and punctuation.

did you know that the biggest canyons in the world are under the bering sea off the coast of Alaska navarin canyon is 60 miles wide thats six times wider than the grand canyon

3. Which are features of a clause?

a. a group of related words

b. missing a subject, predicate, or both

c. has both a subject and a predicate

4. Number these words to show alphabetical order.

watery **wetsuit** **waterlogged**

wetter **water** **whack**

Welcome to my Watery world.

5. Finish the poem.

Shipwrecked on her maiden voyage

The Golden Princess lies

Deep beneath, in murky sand

_____

She gives a home to stealthy fish

Within her timbers, torn apart

What secrets does The Princess keep

_____

1. Should you get into an **altercation** with a barracuda?

2. Place parentheses correctly in the sentence.

After the incident with the shark the one with the mean look on his face, Georgia was wary of scuba diving.

3. Circle the appositive in each sentence.

   a. **Jacques Cousteau, famous oceanographer, was one of the inventors of scuba equipment.**

   b. **Let's get a picture of Will the first diver to get back to the boat.**

   c. **That skin diver, the one with the string of freshly-caught fish, is my brother.**

4. Identify the rhyme pattern of the poem in problem 5.

5. Make an inference about what happened to the author.

As I explored the sunken ship
A flash of silver caught my eye—
A slinky shark was sneaking by,
A creature thrice as big as I,
A creature looking mean and sly.
This morning I can testify
The crusty, rusty sunken skip
No more's the highlight of my trip.

1. Finish the analogy.

   audacious : timorous :: deride: _____

   ○ ridicule   ○ fearful   ○ honor   ○ belittle

2. Correct the misspelled words.

A wistling wich took an ocean voyage with a corus of clever kemists.

3. Circle the intransitive verb.

The barracuda swam away before I could take a picture.

4. Rewrite the passage to give it more sensory appeal.

On her first snorkel trip, Lois was amazed by what she saw beneath the surface. The coral reef was full of underwater life.

Snorkling is my life.

5. Can someone get a diving lesson and a sale price on a wetsuit on the same day at Sam's Scuba Shoppe?

Read

1. What parts of the passage give clues to the author's bias?

2. Circle a statement that is an opinion.

3. Draw a box around a statement that is a fact.

4. What is the purpose of this passage?

5. What is the audience for which this was written?

6. In what situations can nitrogen narcosis occur?

Dive into this story.

The Dangers of Diving Under Water

Underwater diving offers a unique view of a world that is otherwise not easily accessible. Thousands of people take up the sport each year, eager to see the wonders of life deep beneath the ocean's surface. But the thrills of this adventure are outweighed by the many risks to human life and health.

Beneath the water, pressure increases by about a half pound per square inch for each foot of depth. If the pressure inside the body is not equal to the outside water pressure, a diver's lungs can be squeezed and severely injured. This condition is called barotraumas or squeeze.

While using compressed air from a tank, a diver absorbs considerable amounts of nitrogen into the blood. If a diver ascends to the surface too quickly, bubbles of nitrogen form in the blood and can make the diver ill. This condition is known as the bends (decompression sickness) and can be deadly.

Another serious condition, called air embolism, can occur during ascent. As a diver rises toward the surface, air in the lungs expands because the air pressure outside the body lessens as the depth of water decreases. This pressure can tear the lungs apart and push air into the bloodstream. This condition can be crippling or deadly.

Another risk is the danger of oxygen poisoning. A diver who breathes from a tank that has a high level of oxygen can become very sick or can even die. When breathing compressed air at great depths, a diver can also become drugged or sick from nitrogen narcosis.

Of course, in addition to these dangers, there are the risks of accidents, malfunctioning equipment, or attacks by underwater creatures. As you can see, underwater diving is the most dangerous of all sports.

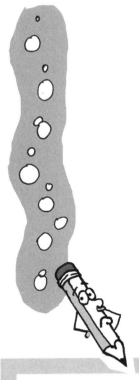

Write

1. Rewrite this beginning for an underwater adventure. Make it grab the reader's attention.

   The weather looked good as the divers prepared for their dive.

2. Write an attention-grabbing beginning for an essay to convince someone to try scuba diving.

1. Identify the mode of writing in 5.

- ○ imaginative   ○ expository
- ○ narrative   ○ descriptive
- ○ personal-expressive ○ persuasive

2. Insert necessary commas and apostrophes.

Have you met Jeremy Mark and Carlos the men who took the worlds longest taxi ride?

3. Give the meaning of the bold words.

I've got great photographs from my safari. I take the most **pride** in the pictures of the lion **pride** we saw sleeping by the river.

4. Circle the predicate noun.

The Radiance is a solar car that holds a record for the longest trip of any vehicle of its kind.

5. What is passage's main idea?

A television travel channel selected the Seiad Valley Café (California) as one of the best places in the world to "pig out." This is undoubtedly due to the Pancake Challenge that the café offers. Thru-hikers on the Pacific Crest Trail can get a free pancake breakfast if they can eat the giant stack of pancakes in one sitting. It may sound easy, but this is a huge stack. So most eaters end up paying the bill!

Just call me flap-happy.

1. You want to find a weather forecast for a city that you will visit tomorrow. The city is 2,500 miles away. What reference source will you consult?

Will you weather the trip?

2. Which pairs of words are **antonyms**?

- ○ abhor – revere   ○ churlish – grumpy
- ○ urban – urbane   ○ mediocre – exemplary

3. Which phrase means **the wheels of more than one bus**?

- a. the bus's wheels   c. the buses wheels
- b. the busses' wheels   d. the busses' wheel

4. Spell the plural of each word.

itinerary _____

chief _____

rodeo _____

yacht _____

5. Add a title to this passage.

_____

On June 12, 1979, a man named Bryan Allen did something no one had ever done before. He pedaled an aircraft across the English Channel. The craft, called the Gossamer Albatross, looked like a bicycle with wings and weighed 75 pounds. During the 35 km trip from England to France, Bryan had to pedal non-stop to keep the craft several feet above the surface of the water.

1. Cross out any unnecessary words.

The first flight attendants, they had to be unmarried nurses who weighed 115 pounds or less.

2. Choose the correct literary device.

Once in a blue moon, Ruben takes a long trip on his unicycle.

a. an idiom   b. irony   c. hyperbole

3. Correct the misspelled words.

benifit   emergency   labratory
restaurant   memorise   allthough

4. What is the connotation of the word ***travel***?

_____

Times a-wastin'.

5. Does the passage give enough information to allow you to make a prediction as to whether or not Wilma will catch her plane?

Wilma's Day So Far

The taxi did not show up to take her to the airport. She caught a slow bus instead. When she finally arrived at the ticket counter, Wilma had a hard time finding her passport. There were very long lines at the security checkpoint. Wilma discovered that she had not taken her fingernail scissors out of her purse. Finally she got through security. By then, she was so hungry that she just had to stop and get a sandwich.

1. Correctly capitalize this book title:

ten places I'll never visit again

2. Cross out words that are not compounds.

passport   discontinued   suitcase
passenger   overbook   seventeen

3. Which example contains object pronouns?

○ Leave the ticking to him and me.
○ He and I will be glad to buy your tickets.

4. What part of speech is the word ***globetrotter***?

globe · trot · ter (glob trot r) n. One who travels often and widely. – globetrot v, globetrotting n & adj

The Trivia Tome

5. Tell which bit of trivia interests you most, and why.

Travel Trivia

- At any given hour in the United States, 61,000 people are up in the air in airplanes.

- In 1987, American Airlines eliminated one olive from each salad served in the first class cabin, saving $40,000.

- At the busiest airport in the world, an airplane lands or takes off every 37 seconds.

- In 1961, it became illegal to hijack an airplane.

Name

Read

1. Circle an alliterative phrase.

2. What is the meaning of the word *tight* in line 9?

3. Circle an example of rhyme.

4. Circle an example of repetition.

5. What is the main idea of the poem?

6. What is one of the discomforts described in the poem?

7. To what common experiences does the poet compare the distresses of some travel locations?

The travel bug calls

Lures to places exotic, far

Places with unveiled mysteries.

New sights, new plights, new promises

All calling your name, calling your name.

But travelers beware, visitors take care,

Dangers, discomforts, distresses are there.

Alaska's cold will grab your throat.

The Sahara will leave you tight with thirst.

Death Valley? Just the name says, "Don't!"

The Amazon sends slimy hissing serpents

to slink alongside your boat.

Write

Finish this diary entry. Begin by finishing the topic sentence with the name of a place you don't want to visit. Then add at least three supporting details or examples.

Dear Diary,
Today while dreaming about places I want to visit, I
suddenly was reminded of a place that I would NEVER visit:

1. Circle the correct word for the sentence.

I (compliment, complement) you on your skiing!

2. Fix any capitalization errors.

Ice Sailing began in holland, spread across northern europe, and became a Russian Pastime.

3. Underline any adjectives and draw a box around any adverbs.

If Charlie had not been such a skillful ice sailor, the accident could have been deadly.

4. Which does not include personification?

   a. Ice climbers scale icicles as sharp and slippery as daggers.

   b. "Come play with me," the powdery snow called out to eager sledders.

   c. An icy wind reached its fingers under the edges of Julia's hat and bit her ears.

5. Read and follow the directions to make a snowflake.

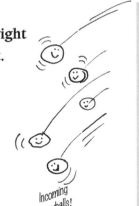

   1. Start with a 6- or 9-inch square of white paper.

   2 Fold it in half, then fold in half again.

   3. Fold this in half on the diagonal to form a triangle.

   4. Round off the wide end of the triangle.

   5. Cut a V shape from the top edge toward the point.

   6. Cut wedges and triangles along the folded edges.

   7. Open the finished snowflake.

1. What is the meaning of the bold word?

Amy is my most jocose friend—just the right person to invite to join our snowball fight.

  ○ competitive   ○ playful

  ○ petulant   ○ timorous

2. Write the **past tense** of each verb.

  think   **know**   **speak**

  lay   **raise**   **snow**

3. Circle the **participial phrase**.

The shovel racer, traveling 50 mph, barely avoided running into that tree.

4. Which of these words would be found on a dictionary page with guidewords *skier* and *snowy*?

  ○ swat   ○ skewer   ○ snowplow

  ○ skid   ○ skimpy   ○ slippery

Incoming snowballs!

5. Write a brief summary of this passage.

Ski lift operators were the first shovel racers. When the ski lifts closed at the end of the day, the operators were left at the top of the hills. Shovels were the handiest things available, so they used them as sleds and raced each other down the ski hills. Now, shovel racing takes place all around North America. Racers travel at speeds of up to 60 mph.

1. What punctuation belongs after this greeting in a business letter?

Dear Dr. Fracture

2. Could you find a **horde** at an Olympic skiing event?

3. Which example shows correct pronoun use?
a. May Dan and me watch you skate?
b. She and Lisa are going to the Olympics.
c. It was her that won the competition.

4. Which are examples of descriptive writing?
○ letter telling about all the sights from a ski lift
○ encyclopedia entry about sled dogs
○ poster telling what a missing sled dog looks like
○ tall tale about extreme winter weather

I'll skate right over!

5. What is the main idea of this selection?

A Breath-Taking Sport

Pair skating is one of the most beautiful of the figure skating disciplines. But it is also the most dangerous kind of figure skating. This is because the sport involves the man lifting the woman high in the air, throwing her in spinning jumps, and swinging her around so that her head almost touches the ground in the daring "death spiral." The moves take great strength, courage, and a whole lot of practice.

1. Circle the prefix meaning *away from*.

mistake   parallel   detract

prologue   anterior   telegraph

2. Describe the difference between **fiction** and **nonfiction**.

_____

_____

3. Which example shows correct usage?
a. You look well after your polar bear swim.
b. It's well that you didn't freeze your toes off!
c. Didn't I do a good job on the snow fort?

4. Add *ed, ing,* or *ness* to each word to make a new word. Spell the new word correctly.

horrify   monkey   worry

silly   lonely   ice

Only an ice cube can appreciate this story.

5. Edit the capitalization, punctuation, spelling, and grammar.

Each year thousands of People enjoys taking a polar bear swim well maybe they don't actually enjoy it but they sere like Bragging about it once they've done it! a polar bear swim is an event where people jumps into freezing cold bodies of water in the winter Lakes Rivers or Oceans they stay in the water for only a few seconds polar bear swims are a very popular new years day activity.

Read

1. What would be the cause of someone having a ski lift ticket taken away?
2. What color and shape symbols are found on hills suitable for moderate ability skiers?
3. What do rules ask skiers NOT to do?
4. Make an inference about what time the ski hill closes.
5. Draw a conclusion about what a sitzmark is and how one is formed.

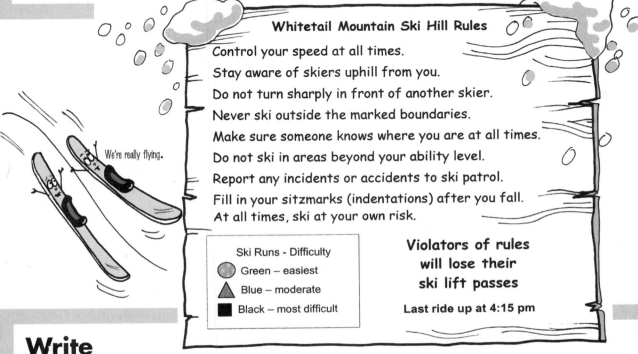

We're really flying.

Whitetail Mountain Ski Hill Rules

Control your speed at all times.
Stay aware of skiers uphill from you.
Do not turn sharply in front of another skier.
Never ski outside the marked boundaries.
Make sure someone knows where you are at all times.
Do not ski in areas beyond your ability level.
Report any incidents or accidents to ski patrol.
Fill in your sitzmarks (indentations) after you fall.
At all times, ski at your own risk.

Ski Runs - Difficulty
○ Green – easiest
▲ Blue – moderate
■ Black – most difficult

Violators of rules will lose their ski lift passes

Last ride up at 4:15 pm

Write

Collect words, ideas, and phrases for a description of a day on a ski hill.
Gather your ideas in the following categories:

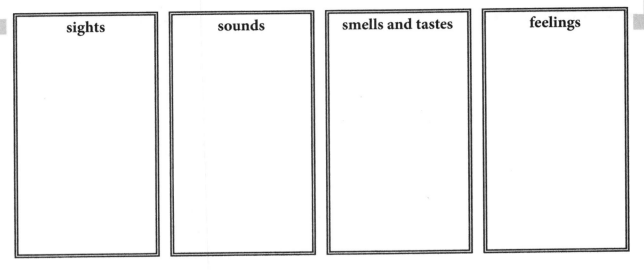

sights	sounds	smells and tastes	feelings

Use It! Don't Lose It! IP 612-3

1. What is the meaning of the word **desiccated**?

The desert travelers came across a small dead animal so <u>desiccated</u> by the heat of the sun and lack of water that only hardened skin and bones remained.

2. Correct the misspelled words.

sissors	Cristmas	sqeeze
neumonia	jiant	cammel

3. Write the past perfect tense of the verb **drink**.

_____

4. What is the audience of the following selection?

_____

5. Write a brief summary of this passage.

The Sahara Desert is one of the world's largest and driest deserts. It may surprise people to learn that this was not always so. Nine thousand-year old cave paintings found in the heart of the Sahara show people herding in an area of lush swamps, fields, and rivers.

I'm waiting for a ride on the next camel.

1. Add correct punctuation and capitalization.

hey everybody shouted the guide look at this 700-foot high sand dune.

2. Circle the error in this sentence.

Roadrunners are so fast that it can catch a moving rattlesnake.

3. Which word completes the analogy?

humid : sultry as _____ : avarice

a. glee   c. greed

b. scruple   d. parched

4. Edit the sentence for grammar errors.

A roadrunner he is a desert bird whom actually belongs to the cuckoo family. You should of seen that roadrunner move at 17 miles per hour!

5. Make an inference about the meaning of the name El Desierto Pintado.

The Painted Desert

I. Location, size
   A. 200-mile long plateau
   B. North-central Arizona
   C. Along Little Colorado River
II. History
   A. Discovered by Spanish explorers
   B. Named El Desierto Pintado
III. Features
   A. Formations – buttes, mesas, pinnacles
   B. Colors –
      1. Yellows, reds, blues
      2. Cause – iron oxides, limonite
      3. Most brilliant at sunrise, sunset

Brilliant!

1. Underline the simple subject.
Circle the simple predicate.

> **Rainfall in the Atacama Desert measures about three-hundredths of an inch per year.**

2. Write an antonym for each word.
torrid   parched   secluded

3. Add the endings. Spell each new word correctly.

regret + ed =   true + ly =

nap + ing =   red + ish =

4. What literary techniques are used in this sentence?

> **Like a thousand angry cats, the blowing sand scratches at my eyes and slices through my sleeves.**

5. Evaluate the passage. How successful was the author at accomplishing the purpose?

> **So you want to climb a sand dune? It won't be easy—because sand just doesn't stay put. Every time you take a step upwards, your feet will sink into the sand. You will stumble forward and slide backward. It is very hard to make progress. Climbing on sand takes a lot of time and energy. Besides the sinking and sliding difficulties, the sand may be very hot. It can burn your feet and hands, so be careful!**

1. Write and define a homonym for each:
duel   flea   hail

2. Add apostrophes where they belong.
one deserts cold temperatures
two camels humps
three lizards tails

3. Rewrite the sentence to clarify the meaning.
Carla rode on a camel wearing a red scarf to keep the sand out of her eyes.

4. Number these words to show alphabetical order.

____ **Caesar**   ____ **camouflage**

____ **cactus**   ____ **Cairo**

____ **cahoots**   ____ **cache**

5. Write a good headline for the story.

> **Travelers on a desert caravan reported a strange site last weekend. A group of 30 tourists riding across a portion of the Sahara Desert stopped for a rest at a small oasis. According to the statements of all members of the party, the water of the oasis was glowing and emitting music. A team of researchers has been sent to examine and verify the phenomenon.**

Use It! Don't Lose It! IP 612-3

Some deserts don't have cacti. What a shame.

Read

1. What is the theme of the passage?

2. What is the point of view?

3. What is the setting?

4. What event in the story is the climax?

5. Circle an example of sensory appeal.

6. What clue does the title give you about the story?

Whispers in the Desert

"Strange things can happen in the desert." These are the words the twins heard before they left for a two-week expedition. They gave little thought to the old woman's words until now. A wild sandstorm had surrounded the group quickly. The fierce winds, stinging sand, and blackening skies sent them to huddle beside the camels. By the time the sand cleared, it was dark. Tom and Tim dug themselves out and found they were alone. Their guide and the other travelers were nowhere in sight. All they could see for miles in each direction was empty sand. They had no food, little water, and no idea what to do.

For what seemed like hours, they sat together in fear, consoled only by the steady breathing of the sleeping camel. Suddenly a little crooked spiral of sand scuttled past, whistling and whispering: "Trust the camel." Again, the whirlwind circled. "Trust the camel," a voice repeated. Tom and Tim looked at each other in wonder.

Strange as the voice in the wind seemed, its message made sense. Tom and Tim scrambled up onto the camel and prodded him awake. Slowly, the sluggish camel struggled to its feet. After some hesitation, he began to move. Trudging through the sand following some unknown inner compass, he moved confidently toward some destination that Tom and Tim did not understand. They just kept remembering the whisper: "Trust the camel." When, at last, the shapes of other camels and people appeared on the horizon, the twins breathed the biggest relieved sigh of their lives.

Write

Write an ode to a cactus. Use the beginning given here, or create a new beginning. Here are some words and phrases to help you get started.

This writing is hot.

barbs	tender, moist flesh
spikes	succulent insides
bristles	sweetness beneath the spines
prickle	like a huge coat rack
cantankerous	a sturdy silhouette against desert sky
irksome	soft-hearted or rough and rude?

To A Cactus

Oh cactus with your thorny coat, your arms outstretched. Are you inviting me to come inspect those fuzzy spines?

34

1. Which sentence shows correct usage?

    a. Tony Hawk is the skate boarder whom has won many X-Games championships.

    b. Whoever wants to learn about the sport of skateboarding, ask Tony.

2. Place a hyphen where it belongs in the sentence.

I really did beat Tony Hawk in a skateboarding competition not that I could ever convince you of that.

3. Make four compound words.

sand_____   _____print

_____back   look_____

4. Moe goes to the sale with $80. Can he afford a skateboard that had a regular price of $165?

5. What is the setting in this passage?

When the math teacher saw that his eighth grade students were losing interest in the geometry lesson, he put away the textbooks. "Here's a problem for you," he said. "Skateboarder Jan does 12 shuvits in a row and skateboarder Stan does 3 cabs. What is the difference in the number of degrees the two have turned?"

1. Where might a skateboarder find a **contusion**?

  ○ on a leash   ○ in the refrigerator

  ○ on a pizza   ○ on his elbow

  ○ in his bank account   ○ under a rock

2. Circle the correct word.

Gina plans to become a professional skateboarder when she finishes (collage, college).

3. Which example contains an **essential clause**?

    a. We interviewed the skater who was wearing the orange hat.

    b. The skateboard, which was lost yesterday, was worth $500.

4. Write two phrases about skateboard tricks that will create a visual image.

5. Read the encyclopedia entry. Tell one way in which wakeboarding is similar to skateboarding and one way it is different.

Wakeboarding is a waterbased version of skateboarding. The board is narrower than a skateboard and, unlike the skateboard, has mountings that hold the feet. A rider is towed behind a boat, riding sideways on the board. Wakeboarders do tricks that are similar to skateboard tricks. They jump off or over obstacles and leap, twist, and spin in the air. The sport is steadily increasing in popularity.

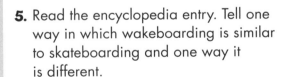

What if you can't swim?

1. Explain the meaning of the sentence.

The new skateboard idea did not work well, so the designers had to go back to square one.

2. Identify the **direct object** in the sentence.

I'd give up my whole allowance to ride your skateboard for an hour.

a. allowance   b. skateboard   c. hour

3. Correct the spelling of each word.

acrabatic   thurough   dynomite

eleet   trackshun   simaltanously

4. Which examples are **similes**?

○ Joe's a streak of lightning on that board.

○ Riding a skateboard is as thrilling as Christmas.

○ The skateboarders look like shooting fireworks.

5. What is the main idea of this passage?

All skateboards have essentially the same components. The platform on which the boarder stands (the deck) is made of wood, fiberglass, or plastic. The board has a tip (front) and a tail (back). The sides are called rails. A set of trucks (axles) is attached to the bottom, one near the front and one near the back. Two sets of wheels are mounted to each truck.

I never knew that.

1. Add correct punctuation.

Though there are many theories on the subject no one is certain about the origins of skateboarding

2. Circle the indirect object.

Susie's dad gave her wakeboard lessons for her birthday.

3. Which word does not belong?

○ defiance   ○ bedlam

○ chaos   ○ turbulence

4. Lisa is at the library. She wants to find a book that will describe different extreme sports. Which kind of search should she do in the library catalog?

○ subject   ○ title   ○ author

Look it up!

Skateboards - A History

5. Identify the bias in the selection. Then write a conclusion for the essay.

City Council Members, open your minds and lengthen your sights. Your hasty dismissal of the proposed skateboard park says, "We're not listening" to the voters who gave you your jobs.

Town surveys show that 80 percent of voters want boarders of all ages to have a safe, confined place to practice their sport. A designated skating area will keep skateboarders off city streets and sidewalks, set rules and limits, and encourage a healthy activity for the city's youth.

Read

1. What is the purpose of this selection?

2. What is the intended audience?

3. Which is probably the most common (frequent) kind of skateboard injury?

4. What part of the body is injured by a snakebite?

5. Is a runout a mishap, a wipeout, or a narrow escape?

Skateboarding is not for the faint-hearted.

Skateboard Mishaps, Wipeouts, and Narrow Escapes

Road Rash: This is the name for the scrapes, cuts, scratches, and other abrasions that result from falls. You are most likely to get road rash on your arms, elbows, knees, and back.

Snakebite: A snakebite is the injury you get when the skateboard rolls into your ankle. This can be mild or serious, depending on how hard the board hits you.

Credit Card: This one hurts. When the skateboard flips the wrong way and smacks you on your bottom, you have been credit carded.

Runout: If you get started on a trick, and you know you're going to fail, sometimes you can run out of the trick and escape the fall. If you are going very fast, you might not be able to run out of it.

Battle Roll: This maneuver will reduce injuries to your shoulder when you fall. If you are thrown forward, instead of taking the impact on the shoulder entirely, tuck and roll right back up onto your feet.

Write

A couplet is a set of two lines that rhyme.

1. Finish each of these couplets.

What a thrill to watch her go!
What a sight when head meets snow!

What a sight when head meets snow!

_____

What a thrill to watch her go!

_____

2. Write two more couplets about skateboarding, in-line skating, snowboarding, wakeboarding, surfboarding, or any other sport or activity.

The skater jumps, the skater spins,

_____

"Sure, it's safe!" claimed boarder Peg

_____

He left the ground; he caught some air!

_____

1. Circle the silent letters.

rhubarb   **wrinkle**   **hymn**

wedge   **muscle**   **heiress**

2. Which sentences show correct usage?
   a. She and he are expert parachutists.
   b. Did Matt and her find parachutes?
   c. Who took the picture of the girls and I?
   d. Lessons cost my parents and me $100.

3. Circle suffixes that mean *one who.*

adulthood   **jumper**   **parachutist**

sailor   **resident**   **piracy**

4. Which piece of writing would be in **narrative** mode?
   ○ step-by-step account of your first sky dive
   ○ essay about the thrills of hot air ballooning
   ○ poster advertising hang gliding lessons

5. Draw a conclusion about how Susan is feeling about her upcoming jump.

Susan recently started taking skydiving lessons. She has been reading, studying, and watching videos to prepare for her first jump. Today at school, her friend Dana notices that Susan is very distracted and fidgety. Dana is surprised to see that Susan has become a nail-biter all of a sudden. She is not so surprised, then, to learn that Susan will do her first jump this afternoon.

I am one with the clouds.

1. Add correct capitalization and punctuation to this title of a magazine article.

the youngest balloonist crosses the continent

2. Underline the prepositional phrase(s). Circle the preposition(s).

On November 1–12, 2003, Jay Stokes made 534 jumps with a parachute.

3. What is the denotation of **tourniquet**?

4. Which is the best key word to use in an encyclopedia search on the topic of the history of hot air ballooning?
   ○ history   ○ sports
   ○ hot air   ○ ballooning

Oops.

5. Edit the passage for punctuation, capitalization, spelling, and grammar.

High Wire Walkers entertained Circis crowds for years sometimes the best performers would walk, without a net below the wire. now many has taken the Act outside the Circis tent. Jay cochrane holds the World record for the hiest and longest high wire act he crosst the qutang gorge in china, 1350 Feet above the yangtze river.

1. Write the plural form of each of these.

scissors   valley   bridesmaid

country   horsefly   great-aunt

2. Jay Cochrane is an expert
high-wire performer.
Is he a **neophyte** in his sport?

3. What does the ellipsis in this sentence
tell the reader?

The instructor had told her, "You
should have known . . . I've told you
not to practice alone."

Look out
below.

4. What stereotype is reflected in this passage?

Anyone with any sense would not choose to
bungee jump. I know for sure that all bungee
jumpers have a death wish. Otherwise, they
would never try the sport.

5. Circle two opinions in the passage.
Underline one fact.

More than 20 years ago, skydivers
began jumping with a surfboard.
They did this because they discovered
they could get more time in the air if
they were lying on a flat surface.
Many new tricks have evolved over
the years as sky surfers have pushed
the limits of their sport. A sky surfer
can travel at speeds of up to 120 mph.
It is the most thrilling of all variations
of skydiving, and it is only attempted
by the most daring of people. Of
course, only expert skydivers should
try this sport.

1. Write the past tense of each verb.

plunge	**take**
surf	**use**
fly	**hurry**
am	**bring**

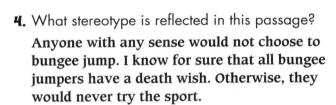
Never say *plunge*
to an airplane.

2. Maxie's mom stopped her from taking skydiving
lessons. Did this **stymie** or **stump** Maxie's
progress at learning the sport?

3. Add **-ance** or **-ence** to each word.
Spell the new word correctly.

○ attend   ○ insure   ○ rely

○ occur   ○ accept   ○ absent

4. Which reference source would you use to find the
current population of Portugal?

○ dictionary   ○ almanac   ○ thesaurus

5. Write a topic sentence for the article.

_____

_____

_____

Eleven-year old Victoria Van Meter
crossed the North American continent.
She did all of the flying and
instrument reading during the flight
from Maine to California. The 4,640
kilometer flight lasted three days.
Victoria is several years younger than
the previous person holding the record
of the youngest female to fly alone
across the continent.

Read

1. What genre (type) of writing is this?

2. What feat is described after the bungee jump with a barbeque grill?

3. Circle two examples of hyperbole.

4. Draw a line under a simile.

5. Draw a box around three examples of active verbs.

The Amazing Stretching Mr. McCoy

Stretch McCoy is the greatest bungee jumper alive. He has defied death thousands of times. People say that his legs are actually rubber bands. They are so stretchy that he doesn't need the usual bungee cord. Once, he leapt from the top of Mr. Everest, dropping all the way to the base of the mountain where he scooped up a can of snow, mixed it with cola, and guzzled it down before being snapped back up to the mountain top. Another time, Stretch jumped from a bridge in the Amazon. He hurtled straight down into the mouth of a crocodile. He bounced up and down five times, in and out of the croc's jaws. On the last trip down, he wrestled the crocodile in a move as swift as a sneeze and left it exhausted on the riverbank.

Stretch has been known to bungee jump while hula hooping, while barbequing a steak, and while playing a piano. It's amazing how he can carry that hoop, or grill, or piano right along with him. You can guess how strong he is. He is so strong that . . . well now, that's another story, isn't it?

Personally, I enjoyed it.

Write

Give your personal response to the passage above. Your response might answer questions such as these:

- **What did you like best?**
- **What techniques did the author use that made the writing effective?**
- **What surprised (or shocked, or disappointed, or amused) you?**
- **What do you think of the ending?**
- **What words or phrases were interesting?**
- **What would you like to say to the author?**
- **What do you think about the character?**

1. What kind of sentence?

The number of bacteria in each quart of backyard soil is 30 times the world's population.

○ interrogative   ○ imperative   ○ declarative

2. Add correct capitalization and punctuation to the sentence.

why are you digging holes in your back yard george asked his neighbor

3. The main meaning or idea of a written selection is its

○ mood   ○ setting   ○ bias   ○ theme

4. Circle the homonyms that were used incorrectly.

Tulip Garden
Open seven daze
a weak
Do knot pick any flours!

Pay attention.

5. Make a prediction about something related to the duke's party.

It rained for three weeks. The duke was so worried that the rain would spoil his garden party. When the rain stopped the morning of the event, he was greatly relieved. There was enough sun so that the blades of grass were no longer wet. Servants hauled eight heavy tables and 40 chairs, and put them out on the lawn. When all the dishes were set out, they went inside to spend the last few hours preparing food.

1. Circle the correct spelling for each word.

terrane   terriane   terrain   terraine

disgise   disgeyse   disguies   disguise

2. Which verb is **intransitive**?

The yard looked too big to mow in one day.

3. Why would these be classified together?

vitality   revival   vibrant

vitamin   viable   vivacious

4. Cross out unnecessary words in the sentence.

I think that it is never not a good idea to mow the lawn in bare feet, in my opinion.

5. About how long are the hedges on the south side of the yard?   *(1 cm = 10 ft.)*

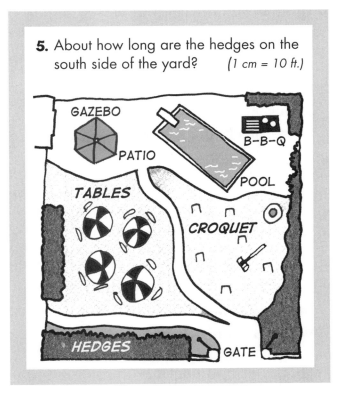

1. Which examples show correct noun-verb agreement?

   a. Several brands of squirrel-proof birdseed is on the market.

   b. Pepper coating on the seeds deter squirrels.

   c. Squirrels don't like the heat of the pepper.

2. What is the purpose of the written selection in 5?

3. Which pairs of words are synonyms?

upbraid – rebuke   **query – emulate**

callow – mature   **brusque – abrupt**

4. Circle the correctly spelled words.

foreign   **height**   **deceive**   **shriek**

5. Number the poem's lines to put them in correct sequence.

_____ **This thing isn't a bird!**

_____ **A birdwatcher, Bertie McBain**

_____ **It's a miniature flying plane!"**

_____ **He exclaimed, "Oh my word!**

_____ **Tracked a bird from Ohio to Maine**

I see!

---

1. Put these words in alphabetical order.

___ **lawn**   ___ **lantern**   ___ **lawless**

___ **laryngitis**   ___ **land**   ___ **landscape**

2. Correct the sentences.

Hardly no one has squirrels in their garden. No chipmunks live there neither.

3. Could **brawn** be an advantageous characteristic for a landscaper?

That's quite a tale.

4. Circle any misspelled words. Give the correct spelling.

The word squirel comes from two Greke words which mean large butshy trail. Squirrells, like other rodants, have teeth which are purfect for nawing and grinding seeds or nuts.

5. Revise the sentences for clarity.

   a. While eating my lunch, a squirrel hopped up on the railing and chattered at me.

   b. We were surprised after the barbeque by the squirrels.

   c. A storm came up suddenly mowing the lawn.

   d. When I came out the back door, I saw a chipmunk eating something out of the orange girl's backpack.

Read

1. Read the descriptions of the folks who attended the duke's backyard garden party.

2. Circle a phrase in each example that represents an effective use of words.

3. Give a brief response to each character, telling why you would or would not want to meet the person.

4. Draw a picture of your favorite character.

You are cordially invited to meet the guests . . .

Count Pompous is strutting about the great yard with a frilly hat and silver-toed, high-heeled boots. He will probably keep his nose in the air the entire evening.

Lady Columbine brashly shows off her beauty and grace. She just knows that you're gazing at her, and have eyes for no one else. But if you are not a young, handsome, and wealthy prince, she won't waste her time on you.

Little Prince Mischief is so small that the guests hardly notice him. He lurks under tables and behind curtains, eavesdropping and spying. Occasionally, he slips a gooey cream puff inside a lady's shawl or tucks a crudité into a tall hairdo.

Judge d' Éclair is a terribly important man. He hovers close to the plentiful food displays at these lavish parties. Oh, how he loves to eat! If you stop to chat with him, do bring along a pastry or two.

Look quickly! There's **Dowager La-de-da!** How honored you should be to come into the presence of this rich grand dame. Be sure you say nothing rowdy or risqué in her presence. She has no time for foolishness.

Countess Dainty dances blithely across the lawn. She needs no partner. I swear she floats just above the surface with her light step. Everything about her seems silky soft, sweet, and sincere. Is she for real?

Write

Think of a character that would make an interesting addition to the backyard party. (It can be someone you know, someone you don't know, or even a fictitious character.) Write a short character sketch to add to the group of sketches above. Describe your character in such a way that other people would like to meet him or her.

1. What literary device is used?

Sweet, slow drops of purple juice dripped from the corners of his mouth and flowed in little blueberry rivers down to his chin.

○ alliteration ○ consonance ○ imagery

2. Write the plural form of each noun.

tortilla   sundae   soufflé   cheese

3. Which shows correct usage?

a. Let me alone to eat my dessert.

b. Will you leave me do this by myself?

c. Don't you wish they'd let us alone?

4. What is the main idea of the advertisement?

> **WANTED:** Live-in cook to prepare five hearty meals a day for local gourmand. Must be trained and bring recipes for rich foods. email: ieat@food. net

5. Write an antonym for each of these comments made about a buffet dinner.

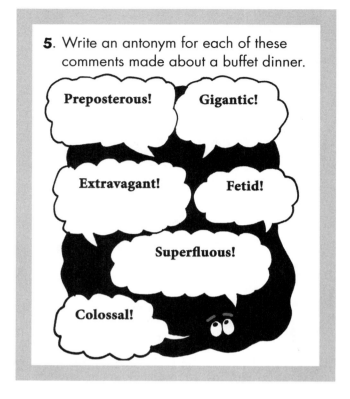

Preposterous!   Gigantic!

Extravagant!   Fetid!

Superfluous!

Colossal!

1. Put the correct punctuation in the blank.

The average person will eat about 60,000 pounds of food in a lifetime____ that's the weight of 30 school buses.

2. What is the meaning of the root of these words: **graduate** and **gradual**?

3. Count the common and proper nouns.

A Frenchman named Michel Lotito has perhaps the strangest diet in the world. He eats two pounds of metal a day.

common _____   proper _____

4. Would the word **nourish** be found on a dictionary page with the guide words **notch** and **nougat**?

○ yes   ○ no

5. Summarize this passage.

Patrick Cunnade of England set a world record for doughnut-eating when he ate twenty 4-ounce doughnuts in six minutes. Others have eaten record-winning amounts of this delicious pastry, too. An American ate forty-five 5½-ounce doughnuts in 17½ minutes, and a fellow countryman ate twenty-two 1½-ounce doughnuts in 1½ minutes.

Doughnuts, beware!

1. Add the ending to each word.
Spell the new word correctly.

pay + able =   carry + ing =

pray + ed =   fancy + ful =

Don't forget the cherry.

2. Name the underlined clause.

<u>That Joe could eat 20 doughnuts in a minute</u> worried his mom.

○ noun clause   ○ verb clause   ○ adverbial clause

3. A recipe for a salami mousse would most likely be written in which mode?

○ descriptive   ○ expository

○ narrative   ○ personal-expressive

4. Write the meaning of the underlined word.

When the main course arrived, it was so <u>malodorous</u> that the princess gasped, covered her nose with her napkin, and ran away.

5. Follow the directions.

  a. Get a sheet of 8½ x 11" paper.

  b. Draw a cone in the bottom third of the paper.

  c. Draw and color a scoop of strawberry ice cream on top of the cone.

  d. Draw 2 scoops of orange sherbet on top of the strawberry scoop.

  e. Put 4 more scoops on the cone. Make every other one chocolate.

  f. Draw a cherry on the top of the cone.

---

1. What reference source is a listing of synonyms for many words?

Bon apetit!

2. Add apostrophes where needed.

Its a good idea to limit the childrens intake of doughnuts in the morning, isnt it?

3. Finish the analogy.

gourmand : eating

as **detective** : _____

4. Find the phrases in the sentences.

Eating pizza is a favorite American pastime.
Americans eat over 75 acres of pizza in a day.

gerund phrase _____

prepositional phrases _____

5. Write a beginning for this passage

Take A Bite of The Largest Cake

_____

_____

This record-breaking cake is a birthday cake. It took 20 bakers over 700 hours to bake the cake and 14 more hours to put it together. With the 34,000 pounds of icing, it weighs 130,000 pounds. So, step right up and have your share of the 23 million calories! By the way, does anyone know whose birthday it is?

Read

1. How many desserts are less expensive than the custard?

2. How much would a customer pay for six doughnuts, a mousse, a piece of pie, and a cappuccino?

3. Which menu item appeals to you most? Why?

Enjoy!

Je suis le meilleur chef.

Chef Henri's Sidewalk Cafe

PEANUT BUTTER-CHOCOLATE SILK PIE	$7
LEMONY CREAM SOUFFLE	$3
TRIPLE CHOCOLATE TRIFLE	$9
SIX SUGARED DONUT FLUFFS	$3
BUTTERSCOTCH POT-AU-CREME	$5
CHERRY-BUTTER PUFFS	$6
MOCHA FUDGE ECLAIR	$5
PINEAPPLE COCONUT MOUSSE	$4
WHIPPED CHOCOLATE CHIP CUSTARD	$4
APPLE-CUSTARD TURNOVER	$6
KIWI GRAPEFRUIT FLAN	$6
FOUR TINY APRICOT NAPOLEONS W/RASPBERRY SAUCE	$7
MINT CAPPUCCINO	$3

Write

Write a phrase to describe each menu item. Try to include phrases that show appeal to all five senses.

Souffle _____

Trifle _____

Fluffs _____

Pot-Au-Creme _____

Cream Puffs _____

Pie _____

Cake _____

Eclair _____

Mousse _____

Custard _____

Turnover _____

Flan _____

Napoleons _____

Cappuccino _____

1. Write a possessive phrase that means

a. the tricks of a clown _____

b. the trick of a clown _____

c. the trick of three clowns _____

d. the tricks of three clowns _____

2. Add correct punctuation and capitalization.

when the lion tamer hollered look out sam was so startled that he dropped his fire sticks

3. In the sentence above, Sam the fire-eater dropped his fire sticks. What caused this?

4. The trapeze act is just about to begin. Is the act **imminent** or **eminent**?

Once I lived for a whole week on a can of sardines.

Wow! And you never fell off?

5. Which examples contain puns?

a. That clown is as cool as an ice cube.

b. It's high time for the tightrope walking act to begin.

c. Pass the popcorn and pepper, please.

d. My stomach is asking for more pizza.

e. Is it true that the lion-tamer's name is Ibenin Jaw?

f. That trapeze artist stretches like a rubber band.

g. The contortionist can't make it to the show today. She's all tied up.

h. I hear the elephant trainer packed his trunk and left the circus.

That's the tooth, and nothing but the tooth.

1. Correct the misspelled words.

**exaggerate   diffrence   immediatly
managable   outrageus   irregular**

2. Circle the independent clause.

A circus train has several kinds of cars, some specially designed to hold animals.

3. What is the connotation of **lavish**?

_____

4. Which information would not be found in an encyclopedia?

○ facts about elephants

○ the history of circuses

○ climate in Asia

○ today's weather in Africa

5. Write three questions you would ask the dentist who performed the dental work on Spike.

The largest dental caps ever made were for a patient named Spike (an Asian elephant). The 19-inch long steel caps were designed to repair Spike's cracked tusks. The surgery to repair the tusks took 3½ hours.

1. Circle each prefix. Write the meaning.

   a. precaution _____

   b. forewarned _____

   c. contradict _____

2. Add capital letters where necessary.

The world's largest animal orchestra is the thai elephant orchestra which gives concerts in lampang, thailand. founders of the orchestra organized the concerts to benefit conservation of asian elephants.

3. Write the correct form of the adjective **noisy**.

Lulabelle is the _____ of the three elephants.

4. Stanley is writing a get-well card. What is the audience for this kind of writing?

_____

5. Write a short summary of the passage.

Visitors to the 1952 Bertram Mills Circus in London saw an amazing and unique performance. It was during this circus tour that Randy Horn (UK) became the first person to throw six cups and saucers with his feet, catch them on his head, and add a teaspoon of sugar—all while riding a unicycle.

Wheeeee!

1. Make necessary corrections in language usage.

That there escape artist, she got out of the handcuffs too quickly. Someone should of made the locks more complicated.

2. What part of a book is an alphabetical listing of terms used in the book, along with the definitions?

3. Circle the words that are spelled correctly.

   brutal   **candle**   **classical**

   mobel   **shrivle**   **legel**

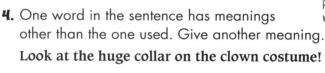

Pack your bags, we're moving.

4. One word in the sentence has meanings other than the one used. Give another meaning.

Look at the huge collar on the clown costume!

_____

_____

5. Edit the passage for capitalization, punctuation, and grammar.

The ringling brothers-Barnum & bailey circus depends on its circus trains to move performers, animals, and equipment. The Circus travel about 16,000 miles each year and moving the circus is a major ordeal. Each Train has a trainmaster whose job it is to keep the trains running well and operating on schedule. The Trains can be 50–60 cars long: there are cars for performers staff maintenance crews technicians and animals after the train reaches its destination it takes 16 hours to unload the Trains and set up for the shows.

Read

1. How long after the first circus in America did the Greatest Show on Earth begin?

2. How many years passed between the first circus parade and the discontinuation of the Ringling Brothers-Barnum & Bailey parades?

3. Jumbo the Elephant was killed by a freight train three years after she came to New York City. What year was that?

4. How many years ago was cotton candy invented?

5. Give the names of two famous animal circus performers.

Circus History Time Line

1793	1797	1825	1838	1872	1882	1900	1907	1920	1938
first circus in America	first circus parade	first circus in a tent	first circus moved by rail	Greatest Show on Earth begins	Jumbo the Elephant comes to New York	cotton candy invented	Ringling Bros. buys Barnum and Bailey	R.Bros - B&B discontinue circus parades	Gargantua the Gorilla joins circus tour

Writing letters is my specialty.

Write

Choose a job in a circus that you would like to try. (This can be an imaginary situation.) Write a business letter to a fictitious circus applying for a job. In the letter, present a good argument as to why you are qualified for the job. Create an address for the letter.

Possible jobs:

ringmaster
elephant trainer
clown
lion tamer
trapeze artist
high wire performer
acrobat
trainmaster
animal feeder
fire-eater
costume designer

1. The point in a story plot where the conflict is solved is the

○ climax   ○ mood

○ resolution   ○ exposition

2. Circle the subject of the sentence.

Did you know that humans spend a third of their lives sleeping?

3. Add correct punctuation and capitalization to this opening and closing of a business letter to a dentist:

dear dr drill

        yours truly

4. Give a synonym and an antonym for the word **arduous**.

synonym _____

antonym _____

I really need a towel after that workout.

5. What is the main idea of the notice?

NOTICE:

To All Gym Members

Due to the increased costs of utilities, we can no longer supply towels free of charge.

New Fees For Towels

One-Day Use - $1

Week Use - $5

Unlimited Use - $45/yr

1. Use your dictionary to help answer the question:

Should you hire a *wraith* to be your personal trainer at the gym?

2. Tell the part of speech for each bold word in the sentence.

Strangely enough, the strongest muscle in the **human** body **is** the tongue.

3. What is the meaning of *impeccable*?

a. indelible   c. immature

b. hostile   d. inedible

4. Correct the misspelled words.

mosquito   **echoe**   **canoe**   **altoe**

tornadoe   **banjo**   **cello**   **oleo**

Dictionary

I could use a personal trainer.

5. Add a title and a topic sentence to the article.

_____

_____

This amazing feat took place in Los Angeles in 1998. The Chinese man lifted a column of bricks that was suspended from a chain attached to his ear. The bricks weighed 110 pounds, making Li Jian Hua the new record-holder in this strange sport.

1. Put commas in the correct places.

On September 30 2001 a team of body builders in Kenosha Wisconsin pulled a 36620-pound truck over three miles setting a world record.

2. Are there any linking verbs in the sentence?

They may look easy when I do them, but one-arm pushups are really hard.

3. What is the meaning of the sentence?

Those pushups you did don't amount to a hill of beans.

Ooof! *Pant!*

4. An advertisement for a new brand of barbells is an example of

○ expository writing   ○ persuasive writing

○ narrative writing   ○ imaginative writing

5. Number the sentences to arrange them in a sensible sequence.

_____ Then he put the car on his head. He balanced it for 33 seconds to set a record.

_____ He set another record in 2001.

_____ In 1999, John Evans took the engine out of a mini car.

_____ This time, John stacked 96 milk crates on his head and balanced them.

_____ This reduced the car's weight to 352 pounds.

1. Write a homonym for each word.

lone	miner	naval
packed	taught	side

2. Does the pronoun in this sentence agree with its antecedent?

Isn't she the weightlifter that set a new world record?

3. In which section of the Dewey Decimal system will you find biographies?

_____

4. Write the present tense of each verb.

hid _____   chose_____

lay _____   rung_____

threw _____   rose _____

5. Edit this selection for capitalization, punctuation, and usage.

some people such as Fuatai Solo climbs coconut trees for fun when he broke the tree climbing record in Sukuna park fiji fuatai was so excited that he climbed the tree a second time this time as he climbed he held the prize money in their teeth

Athletic shoes keep a fitness program running.

Name

Read

1. Who sponsored the chin-up competition?

2. Make an inference about why Uma Glass was able to beat Susie Fisher.

3. At what point in the race did Uma pass Susie?

4. What interrupted Lester during his event?

5. How long was the distance of Uma's race?

6. Compare the information in the two captions and their pictures. Draw a conclusion about a similarity in the two situations.

Lester M. Quivver was well on his way to a win in the City Gym Chin-Up Competition. He had done 57 repetitions when he was interrupted and lost his rhythm. He took third place.

There was a close finish in the 10-K benefit run. In second place until the last 29 seconds of the race, Uma Glass overtook Susie Fisher and won by 0.8 seconds.

Write

Write the missing captions. Use your imagination to decide what is happening, then write an explanation to inform the readers.

1. Edit the sentence for correct punctuation.

The smallest muscles length, is five hundredths, of an inch long.

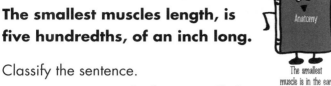

The smallest muscle is in the ear.

2. Classify the sentence.

Motor neurons are the longest cells in the human body it's amazing to learn that they can be over four feet long.

○ a fragment   ○ run-on   ○ complete

3. Ninety-nine percent of J.J.'s body is covered with tattoos. Would it be accurate to say that his tattoos are ubiquitous?

4. Each year for the last ten years, Julianna has added one more tattoo to her body than in the previous year. In 1998, she got seven new tattoos. Predict the number she'll add in 2006.

5. Which sentences contain metaphors?

   a. My toaster plays a game of hide-and-seek with my toast.

   b. Her eyes were purple velvet pools.

   c. Muscleman Matt mashes melons many Mondays.

   d. Life is a gift waiting to be opened.

   e. The doctor's words were unsolvable puzzles.

   f. Your desk is a small version of the Bermuda Triangle; things go into it and are never seen again.

I'm all cracked up!

1. Circle the interrogative pronouns.

who	all	most
whom	what	this
which	several	their

2. Rewrite the sentence with an active verb.

Al's leg bone was cracked by the fall.

3. Circle two words that could serve as guide words on a dictionary page for the word **gallbladder.**

   ○ **gallery — gait**   ○ **gag — galavant**

   ○ **galleon — gale**   ○ **gaff — gambit**

4. Write the contractions.

should + have = _____

they + are = _____

will + not = _____

it + would = _____

5. Play this game with compound words. In each box, write a word that finishes a compound for the previous word and begins a compound for the word to follow.

A. board [_____] way

B. show [_____] stairs

C. over [_____] ache

D. foot [_____] game

E. blue [_____] bleed

F. green [_____] boat

1. Capitalize this book title correctly.

how i endured 970 surgeries and lived to tell about them

2. What can you infer about the person who wrote the book in problem 1?

3. Which is not an antonym for **churlish**?

○ sullen   ○ amiable

○ irascible   ○ grumpy

4. Circle the participial phrase. Draw a box around the preposition.

A doctor measuring sneezes found mine to be faster than 100 miles per hour.

5. Identify the rhyming pattern in the poem. (Use letters such as a, b, c, d, etc. to describe the pattern.)

> I've got a new replacement part
>
> Besides my kidney, lung, and heart.
>
> This set of teeth was almost free.
>
> (I paid ten thousand for the knee.)
>
> My hips are new, too - don't you see
>
> It's hard to tell I'm even me?

I guess I'd better bone up on my anatomy.

1. Correct the usage mistake.

Several scientists says that the femur is the longest bone in the human body.

2. Add correct capitalization and punctuation.

at age 111 james henry brett jr had a successful hip transplant making him the oldest person on record to endure a surgery this took place on November 7 1960.

Amazing!

3. Finish the analogy:

physician : cardiologist as **scientist :** _____

chemistry   physicist   science   medicine

4. What key word or phrase would be best for an encyclopedia search on the human body's protections against disease?

5. Revise the passage so that it flows more smoothly, eliminates unnecessary words, is grammatically correct, and has a clear meaning.

A woman from England had a habit of swallowing things such as hair and she swallowed the largest object removed from a human stomach on record. Having swallowed so much hair that doctors removed a five-pound hairball from her stomach setting a record for the largest object surgically removed from a stomach

Write

Revise the essay. Use the editor's checklist to guide you in improving the selection. Write your final version on a separate piece of paper.

Editor's Checklist

___sentence flow
___sentence variety
___sequence
___interesting, fresh words
___sensory appeal
___an appealing title
___strong beginning

___satisfying conclusion
___sentence structure
___correct paragraphing
___capitalization
___punctuation
___grammar
___spelling

Oh, my aching head.

Read

1. What literary technique serves as the basis for this essay?

2. What does the author do well?

3. What part of the essay is most catchy, funny, or interesting to you?

4. Circle a phrase or sentence that has a strong sensory appeal.

Headackes

I am glad to be a headake. A headacke never has a problem finding a home. A toothacke has to wait for a holey moler. Imagine how confining it is to be a toothacke traped inside a bicuspid! An earacke has to wait for a cold day to chase down hatless children. Even if an earacke is lucky enuf to catch an ear he still has cramped quarters to live in.

Neither has as much room as I have. I dont have too put up with either bad breath or sticky wax. I can find a home in any head that has a problem and most people have plenty of problems! Would you beleive that I have lived in some of the best heads in the world. I have known movie stars presetints and queens and profesional athlaletes personally. I have met more people than any other acke I kno but the person I wish I hadn't never met is the person whom invented aspprin.

1. Add correct punctuation.

**Isnt the largest shopping mall
in the world the one in Edmonton
Alberta Canada**

2. Choose the correct literary device.

**Your expensive new high-density TV is
as tall as a skyscraper.**

○ personification   ○ alliteration
○ hyperbole   ○ an idiom

3. Choose the meaning of the underlined word.

Andy has a <u>proclivity</u> for shopping.

○ large budget   ○ deep spite
○ aversion   ○ natural tendency

4. Write the plural form of each noun.

mouse   ox
antelope   studio
chief   father-in-law

5. What gemstones decorate the dice?

In 1988, a jeweler in San Francisco
created a special Monopoly game. Its
cost is $2,000,000. This is due to the
precious stones and metals used in
the board and pieces. The board is
made of 24 carat gold and the dice are
studded with diamonds. The houses
and hotels are made of solid gold
enhanced with rubies and sapphires.

I'm going to the mall for a fill-up.

1. A collection of maps bound in a book form is a(n)

_____

2. Correct the spelling of these words.

rythm   anser   casle
lafter   lama   ziper

I'm a marathon
shopper's best
friend.

3. Choose the most precise word
to complete the sentence.

**We were privileged to view the world's
most expensive diamond in the world.
The gem was so _____ that it took my
breath away.**

a. nice   b. exquisite   c. fine   d. pretty

4. Circle suffixes meaning *pertaining to*.

artistic   clarify   rivalry   magical

5. Identify each phrase (I for infinitive;
G for gerund, PR for preposition,
and PA for participial)

_____ a. We wandered all day inside
the biggest shopping mall.

_____ b. Marathon shopping is his
favorite sport.

_____ c. We heard about three shoppers
fighting over a TV.

_____ d. Getting the best bargain is
important to Juan.

_____ e. She lives to shop.

1. Circle the correct word for the sentence.

The chairman of the Chelsea Football Club paid $29,884 for a slice of turf from London's Wembley Stadium. This was the (**site, sight**) of the 1966 world cup final.

2. Choose the correct word.

(**Who's, Whose**) shopping bag is this one with the diamonds?

3. Correct the misspelled words.

contageous   courteus   glamereous

malishus   genious   anonymus

4. Which literary technique is used here?

Merchants love the jingling of coins and the swish, swish of credit cards swiping through their machines.

Spend!
Save!

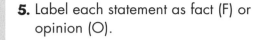
Money talks.

5. Label each statement as fact (F) or opinion (O).

____ A. A person should spend no more than 20 percent of his income on rent.

____ B. The most expensive comic book sold cost $350,000.

____ C. Abe Lincoln was the writer of the highest-priced letter ever sold.

____ D. Joe Pytka paid too much to buy the most valuable edible fungus.

____ E. Antique clocks are more valuable than new clocks.

1. Add correct capitalization.

garth's gold specialties company made a gold mousetrap for dr rodenz's wife.

2. Circle the pairs of words that are synonyms.

plethora – scarcity   veritable – true

acrimony – bitterness   timorous – shy

3. Circle the participle in the sentence.

Exhausted shoppers headed home early.

4. Edit for capitalization.

Who would pay $350 for a yo-yo? In 1998, Thousands of people paid this much for the gold fusion yo-yo. it won the coveted toy craze of the year award.

5. Are these fiction books organized in the correct manner to be found on a library shelf?

Buy me.

Read

1. Give a good title to each selection.

2. Compare the two selections by describing each of these features for #1 and #2:

- Point of View

- Theme

- Mood

- Literary Techniques

Shopping Tale #1

A simple shopping trip for a birthday present turned into a colossal fiasco. Jojo took his little brother Scott along to find the perfect yo-yo for sister Allie. They had a plan to search three different toy stores and game stores. Oh, they made it to all three, all right. But they didn't last long in any of those stores.

At "Toys For Kids," Scott squealed with delight at the tiny action figures and the real swimming pool. All the action figures in the entire store are now in the bottom of the pool. The brothers were asked to leave. The manager at "Toys Galore" is still boiling over the missing hair on all the dolls. However, she's in far better shape than Gretta, the manager at "Games, Etcetera." Gretta is still tied to the video game machine with yo-yo string.

Word spread quickly among stores. No toy store or game store would admit the two brothers. Now Jojo and Scott are home in their bedroom, frantically cleaning up some of Jojo's old yo-yos to wrap up for Allie.

Shopping Tale # 2

Don't ever take your little brother shopping! Believe me, you will be sorry. A little brother in a toy store is like a cyclone on the loose, a runaway train, or an underfed orangutan. No toy, human, animal, or display is safe. He can turn any establishment into an environmental hazard faster than you can sneeze. You may think your little brother is a darling, but don't be fooled. Just walk in the door of any store, any store at all. Things will break; things will fall; people will scream; store managers will call their security guards. Be warned! Be warned!

Let me help you sum it up.

Write Write a summary of both selections.

#1	#2

58

1. Circle the conjunction.

Lou had the winning score even though he made some mistakes in two dives.

2. Cross out the word that does not belong.

submerge	**insensitive**	**championship**
extract	**cooperate**	**mistake**
antitrust	**descend**	**semicircle**

3. Which literary technique is used here?

Cute Katie can't kick her chronic hiccups.

○ A. consonance   ○ C. pun
○ B. assonance   ○ D. satire

4. Which examples show incorrect hyphen use?

○ twenty-three   ○ well-groomed   ○ over-whelming
○ foot-print   ○ all-knowing   ○ U-turn
○ one-half   ○ all-together   ○ forget-me-not

5. What is the main idea of the passage?

The first Water Polo World Championships were held in 1973, when they were added to the World Swimming Championships. Since then, only four countries have won the title twice. These countries are Yugoslavia, the Soviet Union, Italy, and Spain.

Here comes the championship power play.

1. Does the sentence show correct usage?

Do not say nothing about the diver's funny cap.

2. Circle the correctly spelled words.

rasberries	**babboon**	**negligence**
eventually	**exuasted**	**hopeless**

3. The missing words look alike but do not sound alike. What are the words?

At the last _____ , the judges

made a _____ adjustment
              (tiny)
in the swimmer's score.

4. Put these words in alphabetical order.

_____ swimmer   _____ swam   _____ sword
_____ sweetheart _____ swatch _____ swallow

5. At this point in the race, how many swimmers are ahead of the swimmer in lane four?

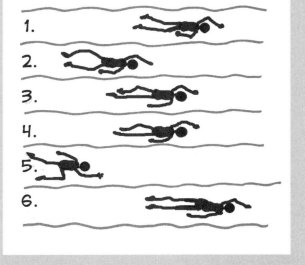

1. Finish the analogy.

lifeguard : _____ :: attorney : defend

_____

2. Circle the **transitive verb(s)**. Draw a box around the **intransitive verb(s)**.

George did so well that the judges gave him the highest marks for his dives. He wore the medal proudly.

3. Greg Louganis (US) won five world titles in diving and four Olympic gold medals. Is it logical to infer that Greg won almost every diving competition in which he participated?

4. Change this sentence into a sentence with a direct quotation.

After practicing for their ocean swim competition, Joe asked Max if he had ever heard a whale wail.

5. Which selections would be examples of imaginative writing?

a. a list of winners in diving events

b. a tall tale about a swimmer with the ability to hold her breath for several hours at a time

c. a diary entry describing a swimmer's day

d. an essay explaining how to do the butterfly stroke

It's a tough job, but somebody's got to do it.

1. What is the meaning of the underlined word?

After a sloppy performance, Cynthia's coach <u>harangued</u> her for an hour, recounting all the mistakes made in her dives.

2. Correct any misspelled words.

leiutenant _____

decieved _____

counterfiet _____

neighborly _____

3. Circle the appositive in the sentence.

The Italian Water Polo Team, winner of the 1978 World Championships, won the title in 1994.

4. What is the topic sentence in question 5?

5. Could the information in the passage lead to the conclusion that the swimmer covered an average of about 70 miles a day?

A Long Swim

The farthest distance anyone has swum at one time is 2,360 miles. This record, verified in the *Guinness Book of World Records,* was set in 2001. Martin Strel of Slovenia swam the length of the Mississippi River from its source to its mouth in the Gulf of Mexico. This swim took 68 days.

Hey, I swim that far all the time.

Name

Read

1. How many of the first ten channel swimmers were not from the UK?

2. What is the difference between the fastest and slowest times?

3. During what four-year span did seven out of the ten make their swims?

4. American Florence Chadwick was the first woman to swim the channel from England to France. She did this on September 11, 1951. How much later was this than the first female channel swimmer (G. Ederle)?

5. Make a generalization about which months are the best months for swimming the channel.

6. Make a generalization about the difficulty of swimming in the two different directions.

7. What is the mood of the diary entry below?

First Swimmers to Cross the English Channel

	Name	Home	Date	Time (Hrs/Min)	Route
1	Matthew Webb	UK	Aug 24-25, 1875	21:45	England to France
2	Thomas Burgess	UK	Sept 5-6, 1911	22:35	England to France
3	Henry Sullivan	US	Aug 5-6, 1923	26:50	England to France
4	Enrico Tiraboschi	Italy	Aug 12, 1923	16:33	France to England
5	Charles Toth	US	Sept 8-9, 1923	16:58	France to England
6	Gertrude Ederle	US	Aug 6, 1926	14:39	France to England
7	Millie Corson	US	Aug 27-28, 1926	15:29	France to England
8	Arnst Wierkotter	Germany	Aug 30, 1926	12:40	France to England
9	Edward Temme	UK	Aug 5, 1927	14:29	France to England
10	Mercedes Gleitze	UK	Oct 7, 1927	15:15	France to England

Write

What would you like to say to the author of this diary page? Write a few comments to her. Also, give Jana some suggestions for revisions in sentence structure and variety.

Comments:

August 28

Journal Entry #13

Today was the 13th day of my swim. It was a hard day. The water is cold and polluted. The water is sticky with oil and other gunky substances. The wind was blowing towards me so hard. I had to fight the currents all the way. I had a tear in my wet suit and the water seeped in and bogged me down.

There were hardly any people along the riverbanks today cheering me on as there usually are and, along with the choppy water, that made me discouraged. Two weeks ago, everyone was so excited about my plan to swim the whole Mississippi River. Now, everyone seems to have forgotten all about me alone out here on the river.

1. Insert correct punctuation.

We ate appetizers salads and pasta then fish rice and vegetables and finally cake pie and ice cream.

I'm first!

2. The sentence below is

a. simple   c. compound

b. complex   d. compound-complex

When Val was a little girl, she fell into the goldfish pond at the May Day party.

3. Is **benign** an antonym for **macabre**?

4. A lady tells a story about events at the World's Largest Maple Syrup Festival. She narrates the story as an outside observer. The point of view is

a. first person

b. second person

c. third person

5. Predict what will happen next.

The ground-breaking ceremony for the new game arcade began quietly. The ceremony was solemn, with builders, bankers, and investors making nice speeches about the value of the arcade for the community. Twelve kids had been invited to break the ground. They waited with their shovels. The signal came for the first boy to dig a shovelful of dirt. He dug; but he could not resist tossing the dirt high into the air so that it fell on the next kid in line. There were giggles from the young people and glares from the adults. The next person, Ellie, stepped up and dug a chunk of dirt, her eyes twinkling.

1. Does the pronoun agree with its antecedent?

Each of the clowns at the event enjoy the cream puffs.

2. What is the meaning of **fete**?

Someone held a lavish fete at the country club.

3. Correct any misspelled words.

chaos	**frawd**	**pauper**
eloquint	**beerd**	**lepard**

4. Edit the punctuation and capitalization.

cuban dancers thrilled the Spectators at the World's largest dance festival over 4000 dancers entertained for ten days at the festival in canta catarina brazil

5. A dictionary lists these meanings for a word. What is the word?

1. A social gathering for pleasure or amusement n.

2. A group of persons gathered together for an activity n.

3. A political group n.

4. To celebrate v.

Samba.

1. Add correct capitalization.

my favorite days of the year are the fourth of july, halloween, valentine's day, any saturday, and any day in july.

2. Circle the correct word for the sentence.

I'm (confident, confidant) that Julianna's party will be a smashing success.

3. What is the case of the underlined word, **nominative** or **objective**?

Right after the fireworks, the <u>orchestra</u> started playing classical music.

4. What is the meaning of this sentence?

You must try eating a whole garlic at the World Garlic Festival. So you don't like garlic?—just bite the bullet and eat it!

5. What is the main idea of the passage?

"Did your snail win the race at the Snail Festival?" Henry asked Amy.

"Oh!" answered Amy, "It was a disaster!" She continued, "Sammy practiced that race 100 times, but . . ."
"But, what?" Henry prodded. Reluctantly, Amy told the story.
"When the bell rang, he turned and crawled in every direction but the right one." She finished, "Finally, he headed toward the center of the ring. But by then, the race was over."

Don't tell me that the race is over already.

1. Everyone praised the dancers' performance. Were they **complemented** or **complimented**?

2. Write the plural of each noun.

radio _____

donkey _____

buzz _____

charity _____

Interesting.

3. Circle the misplaced modifier.

On the morning of the Frog Legs Festival, Erin went into her backyard and found an escaped frog still in her pajamas.

4. Write a memorable ending for a tale about a monkey buffet prepared for 2,000 monkeys.

5. What was unusual about Chef Ibbet's behavior?

Prizewinning Chef R. Ibbet shocked the audience at the Frog Leg Festival cook-off yesterday. He refused to cook any frog legs. Instead, he gave freedom to all the frogs in his care.

Name

Read

1. What does the Chinese Dragon symbolize?

2. How long does the Chinese New Year last?

3. What is the meaning of the word **revered** in the last sentence?

4. What does the passage say that would help you answer this question: Is the Chinese Dragon a creature that actually existed in history?

5. Make an inference about what the Chinese proverb in the last sentence means.

The Chinese New Year is one of the most spectacular and colorful of the world's celebrations. The festival begins on the first day of the Chinese calendar and lasts for 15 days. This occurs near the beginning of February. The celebrations of the Chinese New Year include parades with colorful costumes, banners, and wonderful, long dragons.

The Chinese Dragon is called *Gum Loong*, or *Golden Dragon*. He is a symbol of great power. The dragon comes at the end of the parade to wish everyone good luck, peace, and prosperity. The dragons are highly-respected, mythical creatures in Chinese culture. The dragon is so revered that the Chinese have a proverb: *I hope the child will become a dragon.*

AN ANCIENT CELEBRATION

Write

Examine the paper dragon illustration. Think about how you would make a dragon similar to this one. Write step-by-step instructions that explain to someone how to make a paper dragon.

64

1. What is the meaning of the root that these words have in common?

vitality   revival   vibrant   viable

2. Which sentence has a predicate adjective?
   a. Doesn't that gorilla seem sick?
   b. Which monkey is a trickster?

3. Circle the correctly spelled words.

   absence   importence
   sequence   evidance
   allowence   insurence

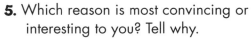

I hope there are no lions around here.

4. Karin is writing a moment-by-moment report of events at the World Camel Wrestling Festival. This kind of writing is

   ○ imaginative   ○ expository
   ○ persuasive   ○ narrative
   ○ descriptive   ○ personal-expressive

5. Which reason is most convincing or interesting to you? Tell why.

Some people are mesmerized by the lions; a force seems to draw them ever closer to the lion cage. As for me, I stay far away. Here are my reasons to keep your distance.

   1. A lion can't be trusted.
   2. The teeth are huge.
   3. A human arm or fingers may look like a snack to a lion.
   4. A lion has a powerful swipe. His paws might sneak through the bars of the cage.
   5. A lion's roar can scare you to death.
   6. Lions have bad breath.

1. Are the pronouns in this sentence used correctly?

Do you think that parrot will talk to you and I?

2. Patsy says her pet pig is *docile*. What does this word mean?

3. Insert commas in the correct places.

Popeye the oldest snake on record died in Philadelphia Pennsylvania on April 15 1977 at the age of 40 years 3 months and 14 days.

4. Number these words to show alphabetical order.

   ____ **gorilla**   ____ **goose**
   ____ **gore**   ____ **gosling**
   ____ **governor**   ____ **gorgeous**

Check this out.

5. Write a short paragraph that tells about the noisiest animal in your experience.

Many animals make noise. Birds chirp and screech, cats snarl, dogs growl, pigs squeal, and squirrels chatter. The world's noisiest land animal makes sounds far more ear-shattering than these. It's a howl that can be heard up to three miles away. Found in Central and South America, this noisy animal has an appropriate name—the howler monkey!

1. Correct the misspelled words.

quaint   quarel   quirkey

quandary   quality   quoteint

2. Which is not a synonym for **urbane**?

○ suave   ○ refined

○ logical   ○ genteel

3. Is the pronoun **himself** intensive or reflexive?

The pet shop owner himself is responsible for letting the African Grey Parrot escape.

4. Which examples include **similes**?

     a. My dog is as graceful as a bulldozer.

     b. Ear-splitting cries echoed across the gorilla cage.

     c. As fast as a shooting star, the boa snatched the rat.

     d. Bats blackened the sky like a thundercloud.

5. How well does the author of the passage communicate the main idea?

How do most gorillas communicate? Hang around a zoo and you might get some clues. You will see, in person, the short low grunts, loud chest-beating, and screeching shouts demanding food. One famous gorilla learned another way to communicate. The story of Koko is well known. A trainer taught this gorilla to express herself well in sign language. When asked if she was an animal or a person, Koko signed, "Fine animal gorilla."

Someday a gorilla may use me to communicate.

1. A new book describes the tricks and travels of an amazing performing poodle whose tricks include untying knots and playing the piano. This book is probably

○ fiction   ○ nonfiction   ○ biography

2. What is the meaning of this sentence?

The lion made a beeline for the poodle.

3. Add correct punctuation and capitalization.

what does the parrot think about the expression a birds eye view

4. Circle the direct object.

Bats detect obstacles with their ultrasonic echolocation ability.

You're on my radar.

5. Choose one of the following topic sentences for a paragraph. Then write three details that you would add to the paragraph.

     A. There are several reasons why a porcupine would make a good pet.

     B. Having a porcupine for a pet is a terrible idea.

Details

1. _____

2. _____

3. _____

Read

Follow the directions to make a frog out of a dollar bill. Start with a crisp dollar bill.

1. Fold the top left corner over to the right edge of the bill. Crease the fold and unfold. Repeat with the right corner folded to the left side. Unfold.

2. Fold the top down so the two corners are even with the bottom points of the diagonal creases. Crease tightly and unfold.

3. Make an inverted fold on each side along the dotted lines of the two side triangles that show in figure 2. When you are done, your dollar should look like figure 3.

4. Fold the top down so the dollar looks like a house with a pointed roof.

5. Fold the pointed left bottom corner of this flap up toward the center.

6. Fold this same flap in half so that the tip points over to the left.

7. Repeat step 6, this time with the right-hand flap.

8. Fold the sides into the center.

9. Fold the bottom up.

10. Fold this bottom flap down at the center.

11. Set the frog, flat side up, on a surface. Glue some eyes on the front.

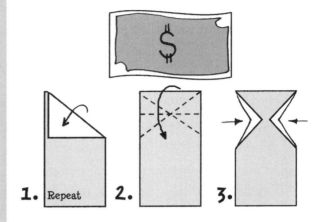

1. Repeat   2.   3.

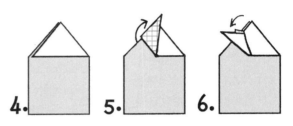

4.   5.   6.

7. Repeat steps 5 and 6.

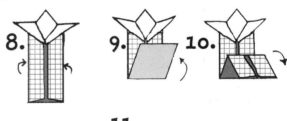

8.   9.   10.

11.
12.

Write

Green is a color associated with frogs and dollar bills. Finish this green poem by filling in the missing lines and phrases.

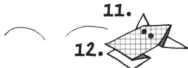

Ribbit.

Green is _____ and _____

The color of _____ and _____

_____ is green.

Green is the smell of _____

And the taste of _____

_____ sounds green.

I feel green when_____

My favorite green place is _____

Use It! Don't Lose It! IP 612-3

1. Give the meaning of the prefix of each word.

autobiography   circumnavigate
midlife   unicycle

2. Show correct use of an apostrophe:

A. to show something belongs to Joe _____

B. to form a possessive phrase meaning **the
ends of two journeys** _____

3. Add the present perfect tense of **dread** to
the sentence.

**Philip's wife _____ every
bathtub-sailing trip he has taken.**

4. Identify the bias of the poem in problem 5.

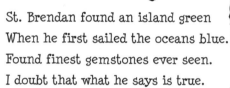

When do we sail?

St. Brendan found an island green
When he first sailed the oceans blue.
Found finest gemstones ever seen.
I doubt that what he says is true.

5. Describe similarities and differences in
the two passages.

    The story of St. Brendan's voyage,
1000 years before Columbus, has been
told since Medieval Times. He claims to
have sailed the seas in a leather boat,
experiencing many adventures. His
tale of a large island with huge
gemstones and fruit fascinated his
listeners. Many searched for the island.
Though some thought it was a hoax, a
modern-day Englishman did cross the
same route in a leather boat. And both
fruit and gemstones are found in
many places around the world—
so why not St. Brendan's island?

---

1. Circle the words that should be capitalized.

fbi   **civil war**
east coast   **middle ages**
kleenex   **geometry lesson**

2. Choose the correct word for the sentence.

**Joe's bathtub sailing trip took him _____
the Panama Canal.**

○ though   ○ thorough   ○ through

3. The denotations of **criticize** and **ridicule**
are similar. Explain how their connotations
are different.

4. On which dictionary page
would **voyage** be found?

5. Edit the passage for punctuation
and capitalization.

**Two Brothers from the U.s.a.
hold a record for the longest
team Motorcycle ride chris and
erin ratay rode 101322 miles
through the Continents of asia,
Africa, north America, South
america, Europe, and Australia
they left morocco on May
21,1999 and ended their trip in
New York city on august 6 2003.**

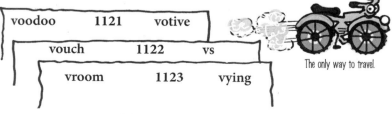

voodoo	1121	votive
vouch	1122	vs
vroom	1123	vying

The only way to travel.

1. Correct the usage:

Where did the skateboard journey start at?

_____

2. What is the meaning of **preposterous**?

_____

3. Circle the participial phrase.

I have some good news about the young man traveling across the country on a skateboard.

4. What is the rhyming pattern of the poem?

_____ Kurt Osborn took an awesome ride

_____ Across the country, so they say.

_____ Three thousand miles, he biked with pride,

_____ Doing a wheelie all the way.

5. Write a brief summary of the passage.

People will try amazing trips in order to get into the record books. They will travel by bathtub, lawn mower, wheelchair, surfboard, garbage can— or even in beds on wheels. One person set a record riding nonstop on the rear wheels of his wheelchair. This was a six-mile trip. If the trip is strange enough and long enough, they probably will succeed in setting a record.

You can travel by bathtub for a clean ride,

or, go in a garbage can if you don't care.

1. Correct the misspelled words.

wiley   **shifty**

luckey   **apathy**

2. Which pairs of words are antonyms?

○ furtive – futile   ○ doleful – cheerful

○ debase – shame   ○ truncate – extend

3. Circle the independent clause.

By the time the storm hit, the bathtub sailors were safe on the shore.

4. Which part of a book shows the author, publisher, and title?

○ cover   ○ index   ○ copyright page

○ title page   ○ spine   ○ table of contents

5. Choose the most precise word to complete the sentence.

C. J. walked 20 miles carrying a milk crate full of bowling balls under each arm. He never stopped. This was a _____ feat.

○ hard   ○ thorny   ○ herculean

○ difficult   ○ trying   ○ perplexing

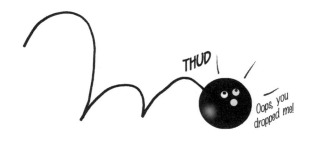

THUD

Oops, you dropped me!

Read

1. Zoey's itinerary is all mixed up. Number the segments of her trip in the order in which they will occur.

2. What can you infer about Zoey's personality or interests?

3. On the tractor trip, Zoey will ride five days, then rest two days. How many miles will she travel per day?

4. Tell what else you would take along on two of the Chicago legs of the trip.

5. On which leg of the journey would you like to join Zoey? Tell why.

I'm packed and ready to go.

Zoey Zach's Travel Itinerary

			things to take along
Jun 2 – 7	Galt to Chicago	deliver pizza by taxi, 2,150 mi	good music
May 1 – 7	L.A. to Sacramento	skateboard ride, 7 mi	clean socks
Jun 9	Across Chicago	run backwards, 12 mi	elbow pads
May 20	Lodi to Galt	turn constant cartwheels, 7 mi	aspirin
Jun 15 – 17	Chicago to Kenosha	push a bed on wheels, 70 mi	ear plugs
May 12 – 13	Sacramento to Lodi	ride in rolling trash can, 45 mi	nose plugs
Jun 30 – July 28	Kenosha to L.A.	ride a tractor, 2,020 mi	thick pillow
May 10	Across Sacramento	walk on hands, 3 mi	blister ointment

Write

Choose one of the journeys above (or any wacky journey you can invent). Write a short argument convincing someone that this would be an important (or exciting, or dangerous, or wonderful) journey to make. Use strong, convincing words and arguments.

1. Create ten compound words that have **off** as the first or last part of the new word.

2. Correct the misspelled words.

An astronaut in nickers had a sceme to rite a book under a seudonym.

3. Circle the common nouns.

The first space tourist took a trip to the International Space Station aboard a Russian Soyuz rocket. The trip cost him 20 million dollars.

4. What is the theme of the passage in 5?

Some stars just shoot their mouths off!

5. What is the main idea?

When I look into the sky and see a streaking light, I always call it a shooting star, but these streaks are not usually stars at all.

Some of the streaks are meteors. Thousands of tiny particles of dust and rock broken from asteroids fall into Earth's atmosphere. They burn up in the atmosphere and streak across the sky. A person might see ten of these a day from Earth.

Some of these streaks could be comets—snowballs of ice and dust that can be miles wide. As a comet orbits the sun, the ice melts into a streaming tail of water vapor, making it look like a shooting star.

TUESDAY WEEK 23 _____ LANGUAGE PRACTICE

Name

1. Is the clause **essential** or **nonessential**?

The closest black hole, which was discovered in 2000, is 1600 light years from Earth.

2. Use the context to decide the meaning of the underlined word.

Al gave sensible and clear details as he described his abduction by aliens. Although some of it seemed believable, I came to the conclusion that it was a specious tale.

3. Write a topic sentence to begin a paragraph that will describe the landing in Atlanta of a large meteorite.

4. Insert parentheses correctly.

After the space trip which by the way departed by accident the space tourist had a long spell of dizziness.

My grandpop fell into a black hole and, it wasn't pretty.

5. Read the encyclopedia entry about black holes to find out why nothing can escape from one.

black holes

A black hole is an area of space made of extremely dense matter. The intense gravitational force of the matter pulls everything in. Nothing can escape, not even light. A black hole is formed when a giant star dies and explodes in a supernova. What is left of the star gets very small, with so much gravitational pull that all of the star's matter is pulled inside itself.

71

1. An astronomer sees that the moon has been getting more full each night for the past week. Is the moon **waxing** or **waning**?

2. Circle the pronouns that are not indefinite.

neither	somebody	ourselves	itself
whom	anything	most	yours

3. Circle the correctly-spelled words.

fourty	people	allready
enough	carosal	cemetary

4. Choose the correct literary device.

   The meteorite was a dragon attacking with fiery claws.

   ○ hyperbole   ○ irony

   ○ alliteration   ○ imagery

5. What conclusion can you draw about the life or mindset of the people to whom the passage refers?

Long ago, the sight of a streaming, burning entity in the sky alarmed people.

The "fire in the sky" terrified and mystified them.

Some feared that the streak of fire was a signal that something disastrous was about to happen.

When a meteorite hit the ground, there was even more fear. Some thought these falling rocks were fire-breathing dragons sent by angry gods to punish people on the earth.

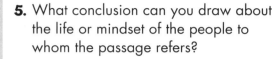
Incoming!

1. Give two meanings for the word **novel**.

_____

_____

2. Make corrections in the usage.

   Scarcely nobody isn't impressed by the launch of a rocket.

3. If you are writing an essay and need a source to provide a wide range of synonyms, what reference source would you choose?

4. Revise the sentence by replacing each verb with a more active, interesting word.

   Interested onlookers saw the launch of the rocket and yelled with delight as it went into space.

This poses a challenge.

5. Add correct punctuation and capitalization to this business letter.

Sue spacey
1313 Corral rd
keno OR 97591

NaSa headquarters
suite iM32
washington dc 20546

To whom it may concern

i am looking for information about Comets can you send me anything

yours truly
sue Spacey

Read

1. How long after the launch of Albert I did the Soviet monkeys set their endurance record?

2. When did the first insects go into space?

3. What year did frogs first travel in space?

4. Which went into space first, dogs or turtles?

5. What animal was launched for the first time in 1972?

Animals In Space Timeline

My travels left me a little space-y.

1946	• Fruit flies are the first animals to travel in space.
1948	• Albert I is the first monkey launched in a rocket.
1949	• Albert II is the first monkey to reach outer space.
1950	• The U.S. launches a mouse into space.
1957	• Laika, a Soviet dog, is the first living being to orbit Earth.
1959	• Able and Baker, two monkeys, become the first living beings to successfully return to Earth after traveling in space.
1961	• The Soviets send guinea pigs and frogs into space.
1963	• Felix is the first cat launched into space.
1966	• A U.S. biosatellite takes fruit flies, wasps, and beetles into space.
1968	• Flies and worms accompany the first turtle in space.
1970	• Two bullfrogs orbit Earth in a satellite.
1972	• The first fish head into space along with the first spiders.
1989	• Soviet monkeys Zhakonya and Zabiyaka set the monkey-in-space endurance record for almost 14 days in space.
2003	• The last flight of the space shuttle Columbia carries spiders, silkworms, bees, ants, fish, and other animals on its mission.

Two hours after takeoff, things had settled down. All of the animals were asleep, except for Mario the chimp who was trained to pull levers. Mario was bored. So he pulled a lot of levers. One of them released the locks on all the animal cages. The fruit flies buzzed into Maximilian the cat's ears. Max got annoyed and pounced on the mice. The frogs ate the beetles, and the wasps chased the guinea pigs. Although the intelligent monkeys tried to shoo all the creatures back into their cages, they could not. Eventually, the squealing and howling, scratching, and chirping woke Julius, the German shepherd dog.

Write

This selection is the middle of a space tale. The beginning, ending, and title are missing.

1. Write a smashing beginning for the tale.

2. Write a memorable ending.

3. Write an eye-catching title.

The racket must have been awful.

Use It! Don't Lose It! IP 612-3

1. Insert commas in the correct places.

Underneath the picnic blanket the ground is thick with bugs rocks worms and sand.

2. Write the plural form of each noun.

basketful _____

family _____

banjo _____

Everybody loves
a picnic.

3. Finish the analogy.

jovial : solemn :: punctual : _____

○ tardy   ○ punctuate   ○ timely   ○ somber

4. Which word best describes the mood of the passage in 5?

a. fearful   c. suspicious

b. silly   d. celebratory

5 In the last sentence, the company president shows some ambivalence. Why do you think she is wavering?

Everybody began to notice the stranger who lurked near the grill at the company picnic. He held a huge platter of raw hamburgers, but seemed to have no interest in grilling them. No one from the office recognized him. He talked to no one. He appeared to have come alone. The rest of the picnickers began whispering and sneaking glances at him. The strange overalls and large hat only increased the mystery. The company president wavered between confronting him and looking for a security guard.

1. Circle the adverbs in the sentence.

Yesterday, the baseball team gobbled their picnic lunch greedily. Seldom have so many hot dogs been eaten so fast.

2. Correct the misspelled words.

The ogers at the monster picnic practised some bizzarre rules of etaquete by playing kazzoos as they ate their hamburgers.

3. For each meaning, write a word with a prefix.

not regular _____

above earth _____

beyond sound _____

one tone _____

4. The book on the right is probably

○ fiction   ○ nonfiction   ○ biography

5 Rewrite each sentence with an active verb.

a. Ants were all over my cupcake.

b. Where is Janie's potato salad?

c. Don't those baked beans seem spoiled?

d. A wild thunderstorm was here during our picnic.

Edwin Err,
World Renowned
HOT DOG CHEF

by Dewey I. Grill

This is a book you
can really sink your
teeth into.

Name

1. Identify the technique(s) used in the poem.

He slurped and swallowed

And guzzled it up.

He slurped down the milkshake

And then gobbled the cup.

○ rhythm   ○ rhyme

○ onomatopoeia   ○ metaphor

2. What is the meaning of **audacious**?

3. Punctuate and capitalize this article title.

what to do after eating the world's largest watermelon

4. Correct the usage mistake.

Those ants they are everywhere!

5. Follow the directions to place things on the picnic tablecloth.

Draw a cupcake on each of 4 gray squares in a diagonal row.

Draw a hamburger that covers 3 gray and 2 white squares.

Draw a hot dog that stretches across some of 3 gray and 3 white squares.

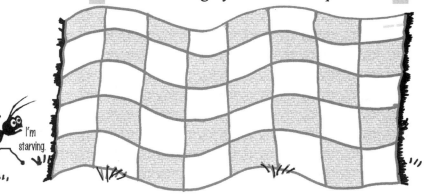

I'm starving.

Name

1. Explain the meaning of the sentence.

When I told Abby my story about the aliens, she swallowed it hook, line, and sinker.

2. Correct any misspelled words.

I just realised that I promiced to bring cupcakes to the picnic. To my surprise, I forgot! I apologise.

3. Write a possessive phrase that means

A. the seeds in a watermelon

B. the handles on two picnic baskets

C. the smell of several onions

4. Cross out unnecessary words.

The abdomen of an ant it contains two stomachs. One stomach is a stomach for his own food. The other stomach is a stomach holding food to share.

5. Write a brief description of the scene in this picture.

Use It! Don't Lose It! IP 612-3

Name

Read

1. What step comes just before baking the beans?

2. Read the description below. What words are used to describe the texture (feel) of the beans?

3. What two ingredients have equal amounts?

4. What metaphor describes the cheese topping?

5. What techniques has the author used in describing the bean dish that appeals to *your* senses?

Is your mouth ready for a sweet but tart wake-up? Let your taste buds be startled and delighted by these incomparable baked beans! Dig your spoon through the cloud of bubbling cheese that hovers over the top of the dish. Dig it down, deep into the caramel smoothness below. Then, with your eyes closed, mound the creamy, honied mixture onto your tongue. Let the maple-mustard-pepper harmony flavors ooze over your tongue and trickle down your throat.

Write

Choose your favorite picnic food. Write a recipe, giving clear directions for making the food. Then, write a tantalizing description of the food.

Give your writing a lot of flavor.

CARAMEL-MAPLE BAKED BEANS

3 LARGE CANS	BAKED BEANS
1 POUND	BACON
$\frac{1}{2}$ C	MAPLE SYRUP
$\frac{1}{3}$ C	BROWN SUGAR
3 T	HONEY
$\frac{1}{3}$ C	BARBECUE SAUCE
2 T	MUSTARD
$\frac{1}{2}$ t	HOT PEPPER SAUCE
1 C	SHREDDED CHEDDAR
	SEASONINGS

DIRECTIONS:

1. Fry bacon until crisp. Drain, cool, and break into small pieces.
2. Heat oven to 300°.
3. Mix beans, syrup, sugar, barbecue sauce, mustard, and pepper sauce in a large bowl. Season with salt, garlic, and/or pepper to your taste.
4. Fold in the bacon pieces.
5. Pour mixture in a deep casserole dish.
6. Sprinkle with cheese.
7. Bake for 1 hour, 15 minutes.

This recipe stirs me.

1. What do these words have in common?

climb   kneel   gnash   psalm   sword

2. Give the part of speech of each underlined word.

The <u>largest</u> landslide recorded <u>in</u> history moved <u>down</u> Mt. St. Helen's at <u>speeds</u> of up to 150 miles per hour.

3. Correct the spelling errors.

mistakes	twelth
unique	lisence
remedie	trubble

4. What literary technique is used in this sentence?

"I'll race you to the bottom of the hill," the little landslide challenged the big landslide.

Some of us just like to let off a little steam now and then.

5. Circle the result in each example.

A. During the landslide, hundred year-old trees were snapped like twigs.

B. The eruption was triggered by a 5.1 earthquake.

C. Fifty-seven people died as a result of the eruption.

D. Mudslides destroyed the foliage which had grown on the mountain for years.

1. Write the correct form of the adverb **deadly** for the sentence.

Though 57 people were killed by the eruption,

Mt. St. Helens is not the _____ volcano.

2. What information can be found on the **spine** of a book?

3. Capitalize and punctuate the sentence.

a group of Spanish tourists led by guide laroux visited mt st Helens after the eruption

4. Which words are synonyms for **inundated**?

○ wandered   ○ overwhelmed
○ derided   ○ flooded
○ frenzied   ○ superstitious

Don't leave me hanging!

5. Add another detail to the paragraph.

The party of ten climbers prepared for a two-day climb. They carefully planned and packaged each day's food. Sleeping pads and warm clothes were packed tightly into stuff sacks.

Just before leaving, each hiker rechecked the ropes and other climbing gear. They said their goodbyes to friends, and were on their way to a great adventure.

1. Does this show correct pronoun use?

Who will climb this mountain with you and me?

2. Which words have a suffix meaning **having the nature of**?

○ childish   ○ comical
○ failure   ○ golden
○ ashen   ○ explosion

3. Circle the correctly spelled words.

convience   efficeint

foreign   mischievous

hygeine   reign

4. Read the passage in problem 5. Predict what will happen next.

Another feat for the feet.

5. What genre (kind) of literature is shown in this example?

**Steaming mountain
Shuddering mountain
Your trembling
Starts my bones trembling.
Your rumbling
Rumbles in my stomach.
Your creaking and groaning
Send my feet flying
Back down the path.
Toward my van.**

---

1. Capitalize the phrases correctly.

**outback steakhouse
my aunt and uncle
pvt. james cohen
a geography lesson
nashville chamber of commerce**

2. Write a homonym for each word.

descent   higher   current

3. What kind of a phrase is the underlined phrase?

<u>Proper training</u> is important for a climber.

4. Edit for capitalization and punctuation.

The Mountains eruption created an 80,000 foot Ash cloud in 15 Minutes some ash circled the earth

Wow!

5. What was the height change in the mountain due to the eruption?

Mt. St. Helens Eruption
I.   **The event**
     A. Date & time: 5/18, 1980, 8:32 am
     B. Cause: 5.1 earthquake beneath
     C. Force and temperature
II. **Effects**
     A. Ash
     B. Deaths
     C. Landslides, floods
     D. Damage to land
III. **Changes**
     A. Height changes
        1. before 9,677 ft
        2. after 8,363 ft
     B. New lava dome

Read

1. What is the meaning of the word **elusive** in the title?
2. Where do sightings of the Yeti occur?
3. How do people describe the creature?
4. Describe the author's bias on this topic.
5. Circle an opinion in the selection. Draw a box around a fact.

I don't see
the Yeti yet.

The Elusive Yeti

You may know this creature as the Abominable Snowman—the large ape-like creature that supposedly lives in the high Himalayan Mountains. The local people call him the Yeti, which means little man-like animal or troll. For hundreds of years, natives in the Himalayan Mountains have told stories about a tall, upright primate-like, long-haired creature that roams the mountains. In the 1880s, guides described large footprints left by the Yeti. Reports became more frequent in the twentieth century, with many explorers searching for the Yeti. Interest in this creature increased when a well-known climber photographed large footprints in the snow on Mt. Everest at about 20,000 feet altitude. Many climbers have reported footprints and sightings of the creature. Others have reported hearing strange calls.

Although one expedition did result in the finding of an unidentified ape-hair, most scientists have concluded that the Yeti does not exist. No pictures or other solid evidence has been gathered. Still, an Italian mountain climber says he came face to face with a Yeti in 1997. And strange happenings are unconfirmed by scientists—especially in places as remote as the cold, high Himalayan Mountains. The idea of the Abominable Snowman continues to be alive and well and mesmerizing. The Yeti inspires countless movies, books, TV shows, rumors, tales, and fireside stories. Certainly something that arouses so much interest and is reported with such frequency must exist.

Write

1. Give your personal response to the selection about the Yeti. Tell what you think, what you wonder, what you would like to see, what you believe. Describe the information that interests you most.
2. Draw a picture of a Yeti.

1. Choose the correct word for each sentence.

　a. (**Whose, Who's**) the inventor of the pretzel?

　b. Are you the one (**whose, who's**) working on an electric fork?

　c. I'd like to meet (**whoever, whomever**) the person is that thought of the safety pin.

　d. (**Who, Whom**) gets the credit for the invention of the stop light?

2. Identify the setting of the selection in 5.

3. What is the difference between an **inventor** and an **itinerant**?

4. Add correct punctuation.

My favorite inventions are these the zipper marshmallows electric toothbrushes and trains

What will they think of next?

5. Write a summary of the passage.

Potato chips were invented because of a persnickety customer at a restaurant in Saratoga Springs, New York. This cranky customer refused an order of French fries because the potatoes were too thick. Chef George Crum made thinner fries, but the customer was still not satisfied. Finally, in disgust, the chef cut the potato into paper-thin slices and fried them to a crisp. He thought this would teach the customer a good lesson. Instead, the customer loved these potato "chips." The word spread, and soon many customers were asking for the hard, thin chips.

1. Spell each of these words correctly.

omited　　embarass　　horid

memmory　stacatto　　paralell

2. Circle the simple subject.

Popsicles, sandwiches, and potato chips were all invented by accident.

3. Tom's invention is **outlandish**. Louie's invention is **ordinary**. Are these words antonyms?

4. What key words would be best for an encyclopedia search on the invention of the Popsicle?

○ inventions　　○ pop

○ frozen foods　○ Popsicle

The sandwich is a happy accident.

5. Edit the passage.

It is said "that the popsicle was invented by axcident." Eleven-year old Frank epperson was trying to make his own Soda pop. Frank he mixed soda powder and water in a bucket the mixture was left outside in a small bucket, with the wooden stiring stick standing in the liquid. The next morning the liquid was frozen Frank picked it up by the Stick, tasted it, and loved it He began to sell "Epperson Icicles" for a nickel. Eventuly, he changed the name of the treat to "popsicles."

1. Explain the difference between **illicit** and **elicit**.

2. Edit the sentence.

Is it true asked Jason that the waffle was invented when someone wearing a metal suit sat on a pancake?

3. Which mode of writing is shown in problem 5?
- ○ narrative
- ○ descriptive
- ○ imaginary
- ○ persuasive
- ○ expository
- ○ personal-expressive

4. Which includes a present tense verb?
- ○ They discovered.
- ○ He is discovering.
- ○ We discover.
- ○ They will be inventing.
- ○ It had been invented.

I come from a long line of famous chips –

the potato chip, the computer chip. and the CHOCOLATE CHIP.

5. Write your impressions about how the author communicated her idea.

The history books show that chocolate chip cookies were invented by mistake—and what a wonderful mistake! Sweet morsels of chocolate nestle in soft cookie dough. When the cookies came out of the oven, the chocolate chunks were solid, not melted. They were elegant in-between warm, creamy nougats that became best friends with the tongue. The chips started softening in the oven, but finished melting in the warmth of your mouth. Thank goodness for Ruth Wakefield's 1930 accidental invention back at the Toll House Inn in Whitman, Massachusetts!

1. Replace each underlined word with a more interesting or colorful word.

Sylvester McClean's new invention is causing <u>big</u> trouble. The <u>loud</u> noise has <u>angered</u> his neighbor.

2. Write two sentences containing the word **charge**, each showing a different meaning of the word.

3. Correct the misspelled words.

resturant   peopel   intresting   freind

4. A dictionary entry for the word unique has this section: [French, from Latin *unicus* meaning only, sole]. What does this tell about the word?

5. Which examples have linking verbs?
- a. Charlie's invention looks comical.
- b. This invention cracks me up!
- c. Which of these contraptions works?
- d. That seems like a mistake.
- e. Is the lollipop maker a new idea?

Write on.

Read

1. Number the headlines to show the order in which they occured.

2. Which discoveries or inventions seem to have happened accidentally?

3. What discovery do you think was connected to the falling apple?

4. What might the 1930 invention have been?

5. What might the 1920 discovery have been?

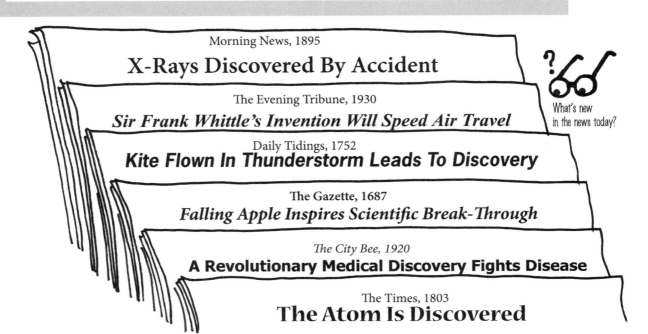

Morning News, 1895
X-Rays Discovered By Accident

The Evening Tribune, 1930
Sir Frank Whittle's Invention Will Speed Air Travel

Daily Tidings, 1752
Kite Flown In Thunderstorm Leads To Discovery

The Gazette, 1687
Falling Apple Inspires Scientific Break-Through

The City Bee, 1920
A Revolutionary Medical Discovery Fights Disease

The Times, 1803
The Atom Is Discovered

What's new
in the news today?

Write Write a headline for each article.

Morning News, 1849

_____

Walter Hunt, a mechanic from New York has patented a new invention. The builder of America's first sewing machine has invented the safety pin, a fastening pin that can hold many things together with ease. Hunt is the inventor of many gadgets, including a knife sharpener, artificial stone, ice ploughs, and a street car bell.

Morning News, 1846

_____

Surgery will no longer be painful, thanks to a wonderful new invention. American dentist William Morton has discovered a way to put patients to sleep while they undergo medical procedures. Medicines called anesthetics, put patients into a sleep-like state where they do not feel the pain.

Morning News, 1956

_____

A new invention makes it easy to fix mistakes. A Dallas secretary mixed up a batch of liquid paper (known as "mistake out" or "white out" and created a substance that can cover up mistakes made on a typewriter. The concoction is a mixture of paint that can be brushed over the mistake.

1. Change this into a complete sentence.

The world's largest Popsicle, containing enough liquid to make 250,000 ice cubes and weighing 17,450 pounds.

2. Create six compound words that contain the word **over**.

3. Write the plural of each noun.

| pizza | fox | goose | jealousy |
| veto | wife | child | trousers |

4. The atmosphere or feeling that a writer creates in a story is the

○ plot   ○ theme   ○ point of view
○ setting ○ mood   ○ characterization

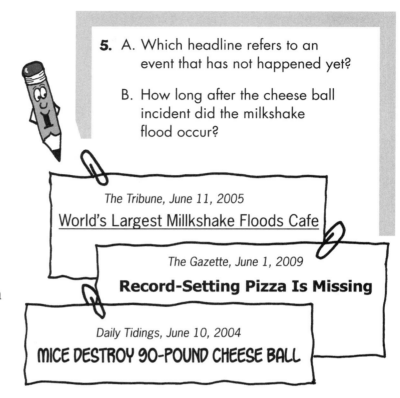

5. A. Which headline refers to an event that has not happened yet?

B. How long after the cheese ball incident did the milkshake flood occur?

The Tribune, June 11, 2005

World's Largest Milkshake Floods Cafe

The Gazette, June 1, 2009

Record-Setting Pizza Is Missing

Daily Tidings, June 10, 2004

MICE DESTROY 90-POUND CHEESE BALL

1. What does this sentence mean?

The prizewinner seemed like an upstanding citizen, but we heard that he had some skeletons in his closet.

2. Punctuate the sentence correctly.

Joe took one look at the worlds largest donut and yelled I want a bite

Don't open this door!

3. Circle the subordinate clause.

To measure the largest dog biscuit I will need something longer than a ruler.

4. Are these words in alphabetical order?

half, **halves,** halt, halter, Hamburg, hamburger, Hamilton, hams

5. Eliminate any unnecessary words or phrases.

A Pasadena, California donut maker created the world's largest biggest donut. Winchell's House of Donuts in Pasadena, California baked a giant apple fritter that weighed 5000 pounds in weight and measured 95-feet diameter across the center of the donut.

83

1. Give the meaning of the root of each word.

inedible   rotisserie   dormitory

2. Correct any misspelled words.

A gentelman from India husked a cocanut with his teeth. The shaggy fruit had a curcumferance of 30.7 inches and wieghed 4.744 kilagrams. No wonder he has false teeth.

3. Does the subject agree with the verb?

The heaviest of all pineapples weigh 17 pounds.

4. Identify the sense to which each phrase appeals.

a. **warm, moist gingerbread**

b. **kitchen thick with cabbage steam**

c. **tart lemon juice brings tears to my eyes**

5. Read the phrases in 4. Examine the topic, word use, structure, and effect.

A. **Describe two things that the phrases have in common.**

B. **Tell one way the structure of C is different than the structure of A.**

C. **Describe a difference between A and B.**

D. **Which phrase is more active?**

1. Identify the tense of each verb in the sentences.

Bernard wondered if his pumpkin would break any records. He still wonders.

Oops, I broke the wrong record.

2. Insert commas where they belong.

Alfred J. Cobb grower of the heaviest cucumber won an award in September 2003.

3. A reference book of interesting and important statements is

○ a thesaurus   ○ a glossary

○ an almanac   ○ a quotation index

4. Sam can't stop cultivating huge vegetables. He just loves watching them grow. Is this a **mania** or a **phobia**?

5. Add a topic sentence.

This giant popcorn ape was created to honor the 70th anniversary of the original King Kong film (released in 1933). It is not surprising that this 13-foot tall, 9-foot wide sculpture of the Hollywood icon set a new world record.

Read

1. What is the main idea of the selection?

2. What is the intended audience?

3. What is the purpose of the selection?

4. Circle an example of personification.

5. Approximately how many scoops of ice cream were used per mile?

That's a whole lot of bananas.

Come see the

World's Largest Banana Split

- Four and one-half miles long
- 6,000 scoops of double vanilla ice cream
- 24,000 fresh, sliced, bananas
- 24,000 soft, red maraschino cherries
- 1,000 pounds of crunchy walnut pieces

A delight of icy cream drizzled with streams of chocolate sauce, proudly wearing puffy hats of sweet marshmallow cream, sprinkled with nuts, decorated with plump, mouth-watering cherries.

One spoonful for each visitor

Made with loving care by the residents of Selinas Grove, Pennsylvania April 30, 1988

Stretches all along Market St.

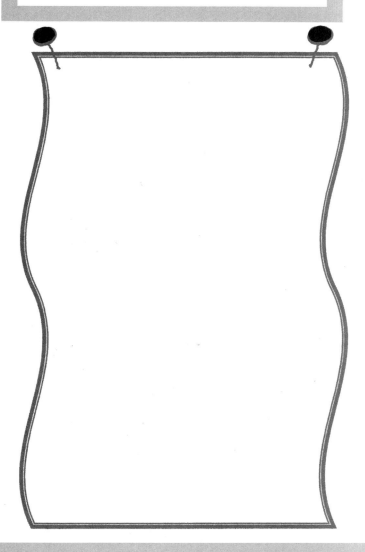

Write

Think of a record-setting creation that you would like to see (or eat). Use the banner to write about the wonders of this food. Write words, phrases, or short sentences to show off the food.

1. Finish the analogy.

backboard : board :: _____ : storm

2. Circle letters that should be capitals.

the boston celtics is the national basketball league team that has won the most championships.

3. Circle the predicate nouns.

Shaquille O'Neal is a talented player. For years he was an L.A. Laker. On the court, he looks massive.

Look out below.

4. An editorial giving reasons that the city should build a new basketball arena is

○ imaginative writing   ○ persuasive writing

○ narrative writing   ○ expository writing

5. Number the lines in a logical sequence with an abcb rhyming pattern.

___ She dribbled back and forth and back

___ And shot it through the hoop.

___ Around the back and down the side

___ Ran around a loop.

___ Across the court and up the center

___ She ran in circles, ran in squares,

___ She doubled back and charged inside

___ She dribbled near and far and wide.

1. Choose a synonym for the underlined word.

The new guard on the team has attended the <u>requisite</u> number of practices.

○ minimum   ○ required   ○ greatest

2. Correct any misspelled words.

That player is admirable, commendable, lovible, reliable, and sensibal.

3. Rewrite the sentences with active verbs.

After the game, Veronica felt proud. All the coaches seem annoyed.

4. Write a good introduction for an interview with the man who holds the world record for spinning the most basketballs at one time.

I'm better at drooling than dribbling.

5. Give the dictionary page for each of these words.

drama   dowse   dribble   dread

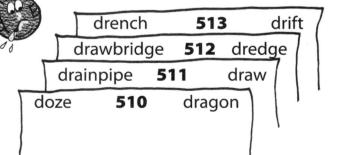

drench	513	drift
drawbridge	512	dredge
drainpipe	511	draw
doze	510	dragon

Name

1. Add correct punctuation.

A Romanian-born basketball player who is 91 inches tall is the tallest man to play in the National Basketball League

2. Circle the direct object(s). Draw a box around any indirect object(s).

After we shouted cheers and built a human pyramid, we threw our pompons into the crowd.

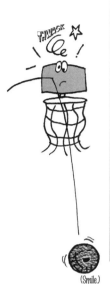
(Smile.)

3. What are the meanings of the two italic words in the passage in 5?

4. Write an alliterative sentence using some of these words.

bumbling	basket	Bruno
ball	barely	beat
buddies	Boston	bruised

5. Make an inference about what has happened to cause the mood or behavior of Player Number Eight.

Player Number Eight sat alone on the end of the bench. He had a towel draped over his head; his shoulders drooped, and he wore a *sullen* glare. His teammates on the floor were performing spectacularly. They stole the ball over and over, scoring 12 points in a row. Still he sat, almost motionless. Now and then he gave a *pretense* of excitement for the team by clapping weakly. For the most part, however, he stayed in his gloomy mood for the rest of the game.

Name

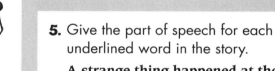

1. Change each verb to past tense.

mystify	envy	pay
defy	worry	play

2. Find a pair of homonyms to complete the sentence.

Did the _____ _____
            (body part)   *(get better)*
before the championship game?

3. Abby read about a basketball player who had shoes that enabled her to leap 20–30 feet into the air. This tale is probably

  ○ fiction   ○ nonfiction   ○ biography

4. Write a great title for the story described above in problem 3.

5. Give the part of speech for each underlined word in the story.

A <u>strange</u> thing happened at the Rosebury <u>High</u> School basketball game last night. Just before half time, the lights went off. They were not off <u>very</u> long. But when they came back on, every basketball in the gym had <u>disappeared</u>. Officials, players, coaches, and students searched <u>under</u> the bleachers. Referees <u>hurriedly</u> unlocked the equipment <u>room</u> to get more balls. There were <u>none</u> to be found.

Name

Read

1. What is the area of a basketball court?

2. Describe three different ways a player could score 12 points.

3. What would probably happen if there were 13 players on the floor at one time?

4. Describe the purpose and the likely audience of the selection.

5. At what point does a player "foul out"?

Some Basketball Facts

- A basketball basket is a bottomless white cord net suspended from a circular metal rim.
- The rim is 18 inches in diameter.
- The basket is suspended ten feet above the floor.
- The backboard of the basket is a fiberglass or wood rectangle.
- A basketball court is about 50 feet wide and 92 feet long.
- The floor is usually made of hardwood.
- During the game, players use an inflated ball made of leather or rubber.
- The object of the game is to score points by shooting the ball through the basket while keeping the other team from scoring.
- Each team has five players on the floor at one time.
- Players may dribble the ball as they move and shoot toward the basket or pass the ball to one another.
- Players may not run with the ball or kick the ball.
- Points can be scored by field goals (two points or three points) and by free throws (one point per successful throw).
- A game has quarters or halves, with the total time being 32–40 minutes of play.
- Players may not push, shove, or grab other players. Certain kinds of contact between players can result in a foul on a player or team.
- When a player is fouled by another player, the player fouled gets to shoot a free shot from the foul line.
- When a player gets five fouls (six in the NBA), he or she is out of the game.

Write

1. Collect words that you can use to write a rhyming poem about basketball. Make one list that rhymes with each of these words: **gym, ball, team, win, hoop, toss, drop, run, score, lose, game**.

2. Write lines ending in these words and move them around until you have created a poem of four lines or more.

1. Which word does not belong?

○ staccato   ○ ricotta

○ legato   ○ piano

2. Circle the prepositions in the sentence.

If you search around the world for the largest jukebox, you will find it in Tokyo.

3. Spell these words correctly.

annaversary   **anonamous**

Antartica   **archatect**

4. Everyone who listens to rock music is a bad influence. They all dye their hair orange, and get many piercings and tattoos. Without exception, they lead unhealthy lifestyles.

The above passage is an example of

○ metaphor   ○ narration   ○ personification

○ stereotype   ○ irony   ○ foreshadowing

5. What conclusion can you draw about James Kirkman from this passage?

In 1987, James Kirkman bought a music manuscript at Sotheby's Auction in London, UK. He paid $4.1 million for a volume of nine complete Mozart symphonies. These were certified to have been written in Mozart's own handwriting. This was the highest price ever paid for a music manuscript.

I prefer Mozart, mostly.

1. What is the meaning of the underlined term?

Had he not been assured that the manuscript was a <u>bona fide</u> Mozart original, the buyer would never have paid four million dollars for it.

2. Circle letters that should be capitals.

shania twain is sometimes called

the queen of country music.

Her album, *come on over,*

sold 30 million copies.

3. Circle the infinitive.

Julia decided to buy the *Legend* album.

4. What is the purpose of an encyclopedia entry about Ricky Brown?

5. Ricky Brown of the U.S. holds an interesting musical record. He is the world's fastest rapper. In 2005, he recorded a rap called "No Clue." For this, he rapped 723 syllables in 51.27 seconds. That's about 14 syllables a second!

You pluck the strings of my heart.

Write a sentence or two of rap. Try to include at least 25 syllables. Then, get a stopwatch or clock with a second hand, and see how fast you can say them.

1. The country tune elicits visions of cowboys and broken hearts. Does it **invoke** or **evoke** images?

2. Choose the correct word for the sentence.

   Her mother's warnings to turn down the volume had no (**affect, effect**) on Gina's behavior.

3. Circle the misplaced modifier. Re-write the sentence to clarify the meaning.

   By mistake, Joe dropped the music he had written in the garbage can.

4. What is the main idea of the poem in problem 5?

5. What is the rhyme pattern of this lyric?

   I walk around the house to find
   Your boots aren't on the floor.
   I search the basement and garage.
   The facts I can't ignore.
   Your clothes are gone, your car is gone
   You're not just at the store.
   I cry because you left me,
   Then I hear you at the door.
   I'm running toward the door!

I'm so touched.

1. Punctuate the sentence correctly.

   Legend a music album by Jamaican Bob Marley is the best-selling reggae album of all time

2. Is this the **connotation** or the **denotation** of the word **music**?

   the science or art of ordering tones in succession and in combination to produce a composition having unity

3. Which examples show correct usage?

   A. That drummer plays badly.
   B. It's too bad that the drummer is sick.
   C. Is the drummer feeling badly today?
   D. The whole band played bad today.

4. Edit the capitalization, punctuation, and spelling in problem 5.

5. Is it true to say that Jerry Garcia's guitar sold for almost $200,000 more than the total of the other items?

That is noteworthy.

Expensive Pop Music Memorabilia

Original Owner, Item	Selling Price
John Lennons 1965 rolls roice,	$229900.
jerry garcia's electric Gutar,	$957,500.
elvis presleys gutar,	$180000.
charlie parkers saxaphone	$144,925.
buddy Holly's electric Gutar	$110000.

Name

Read

1. Describe the audience for whom this program was written.

2. Describe the purpose of the program.

3. How many acts perform before the Lava-Ettes?

4. Charlie arrived at the concert at 11:15 pm. Is it likely that he missed Rocky & The Marbles?

5. Describe your reaction to this concert schedule.

Write

1. Design a CD cover for a live album from the concert.

2. Write a short biography for one of the performers.

Town Center
Rock Concert
10 pm - midnight
Program

Be A Little Boulder, Honey
Curt McCove

Please Don't Take Me For Granite, Baby
The Standing Stones

I'm Yours Till the Volcano Erupts
The Lava-ettes

Intermission

Your Love Is Like A Sabre-Tooth Tiger
Terri Dactyl & The Hot Rocks

I Feel LIke A Rockslide Covered My Heart
Smashing Limestones

I've Cried Pebbles Over You
Rocky & The Marbles

Your Heart's Made Of Petrified Wood
Mick Jagged & The Rolling Boulders

Biography:

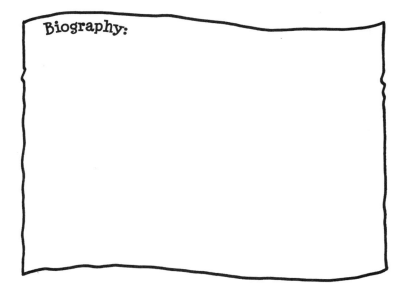

1. Circle the words containing a silent letter.

The reporter stood dumbstruck looking at a scene of houses on the ledge of a chasm and gnarled trees wedged between blocks of a shattered bridge.

2. What is the meaning of this sentence?

The weather service jumped the gun when it issued the tornado warning.

3. Choose the correct label for this sentence.

When tornado season arrives, we put flashlights in the basement and stock up on food and water.

　　　○ compound　　　　○ complex
　　　　　○ compound-complex

4. A reporter stands in front of a TV camera describing everything that is happening as the camera films a hurricane swirling around the reporter. What would be the point of view of this report?

5. Why are the cows in the treetops?

Thursday's tornado actually picked up a herd of cows and left them stranded in trees. Thankfully, the treetops were sturdy enough to hold the cows.

1. Circle letters that should be capitals.

colombian coffee
mother nature
renaissance art
sir frances frieze

2. How many adjectives are in the sentence?

The fastest winds in the solar system blow fiercely at 1,500 miles per hour.

3. What is the meaning of the word **adroit**?

4. Which words would be found on a dictionary page with guide words **tornado** and **toss-up**?

　○ torment　　○ topiary　　○ torpedo
　○ torrid　　　○ total　　　○ torque

5. Rewrite the passage to eliminate excess ideas or words.

There is an area in the United States named "Tornado Alley." This is called "Tornado Alley" because the conditions in the area are just right for spawning tornados. In the U.S., tornados form in places where there is a lot of moist, wet warm air in huge amounts from the Gulf of Mexico. That is what is necessary for a tornado to form.

1. Which words are antonyms for **monumental**?

○ infinitesimal   ○ obstreperous   ○ miniscule

2. Circle the clause in the sentence. Tell what kind of clause it is.

That's the worst storm that I have seen in this area so far.

3. Correct the misspelled words.

decision   musichian

frivolus   ingeneous

A bad storm can turn you inside out.

4. Which examples contain a simile?

a. My little brother is a raging tornado.

b. I'm buried in a blizzard of homework.

c. Taking a math test is like having a tooth pulled.

d. Writing a poem is like trying to stand up in a windstorm.

5. Label each sentence in the paragraph **F** for fact or **O** for opinion.

Tornados form where there are large, quickly-rising swells of warm, moist air. The movement of the air upwards causes a rotation. When the air rotates intensely, it turns into a tornado—a spiraling, whirling mass. If you are smart, you will have removed yourself from the area before this happens. In fact, if you are really smart, you will stay completely away from areas where tornados can develop.

1. Write the sentence correctly.

I don't know of no area that gets more snowfall than Mt. Rainier, Washington.

Good advice.

2. Write a word (with a prefix) meaning

A. to act between

B. not typical

C. having equal sides

3. Correct the capitalization and punctuation.

The greatest depth of snow measured was found at tamarac California usa the measurement was taken in march 1911.

4. Write a paraphrase of the information in 5.

5. Where is the best place to be outdoors during a tornado?

Tornado Safety Tips

Keep a supply of food, water, batteries, bedding, and flashlights in your basement or first floor.

If you see a tornado coming or hear a warning signal, take cover immediately.

Take shelter in the lowest part of a building.

Stay away from doors and windows.

Do not stay in your car.

If you are outside, get under a bridge or in a ditch.

Use It! Don't Lose It! IP 612-3

Read

1. What percentage of the continent of Australia gets less than ten inches of rain a year?
   a. about 10%   b. less than 50%   c. more than 50%   d. exactly 50%

2. Is the east coast of Australia one of the wetter or drier areas of the continent?

3. Which cities receive more rain in a year than Sydney?

4. Draw a conclusion about the amount of rain in the northern part of the continent
   (in comparison to the southern part).

5. What is the meaning of the stripes on the map?

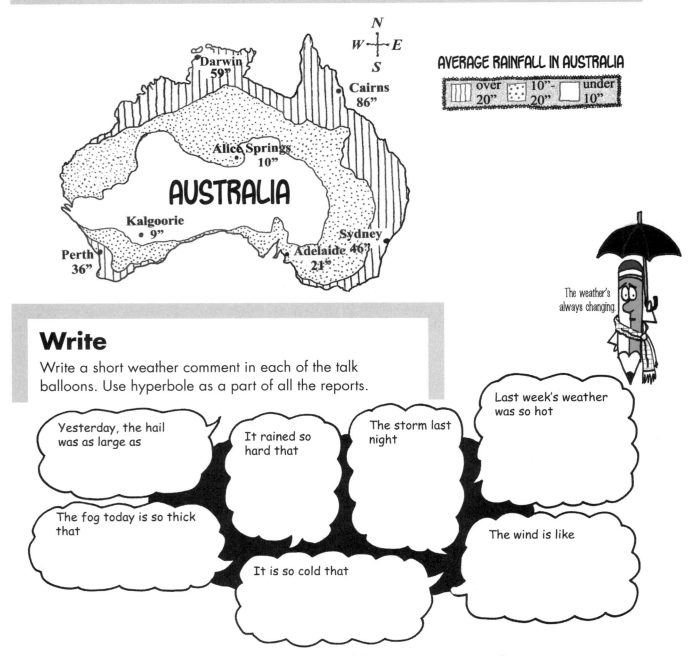

Write

Write a short weather comment in each of the talk
balloons. Use hyperbole as a part of all the reports.

Yesterday, the hail
was as large as

It rained so
hard that

The storm last
night

Last week's weather
was so hot

The fog today is so thick
that

It is so cold that

The wind is like

1. Find a pair of homonyms to fill the blanks.

This is the _____ time the
newspaper carrier has ventured _____
in a blizzard.
(out)

2. Does the pronoun agree with the antecedent?

Both the milkman and the paper carrier are late today. I wonder if the storm is holding him up.

3. The approach a writer takes toward a topic or the attitude the writer has toward a topic is the

○ mood   ○ theme   ○ tone

4. Finish the chart to show the tenses.

present	lie	lay
present participle	(is)	(is)
past		
past participle	(has)	(has)

5. Follow the directions to make a hat from a newspaper page.

    A. Place the newspaper on a table with the longest edge up and down.

    B. Bring the top edge down to fold the page in half.

    C. Fold the top right corner in to make a triangle. Repeat with the top left edge.

    D. Fold the bottom flap up to touch the bottom edge of the triangles.

    E. Flip the shape over and fold the other bottom edge up.

    F. Use markers or crayons to add decorations to the hat.

 *Don't wear a newspaper hat in the rain.*

1. The reporter gave evidence that the mayor's claims about a new bridge were not justified. Did the reporter **refute** or **deny** the mayor's claims?

2. Insert commas in the correct places.

The editor on the other hand argued in favor of the plan for a new bridge.

3. Give the case of the underlined noun.

A reporter interviewed all nine <u>candidates</u> for the mayoral position.

Luckily, I come with an eraser.

4. Rearrange the passage to make sense.

After finishing both crossword puzzles, Anne decides to try the tongue twister. When she finishes the pun cipher, she starts on the first crossword puzzle. Anne does all the puzzles in the paper every day.

5. Can you tell how many puzzles are included in this newspaper?

Puzzle Index
Thursday, Nov. 30
    I. Crossword puzzles
        A. Easy, p. 17
        B. Hard, p. 35
    II. Ciphers
        A. Quotations, p. 35
        B. Puns, p. 12 and 19
        C. Tongue Twisters, p. 19
    III. Anagrams, pgs. 17 and 44
    IV. Word search, p. 44

1. Circle correctly-spelled words.

radical   **vessle**   **frugel**   **legel**

candel   **spiral**   **cynicle**   **model**

2. Write possessive phrases to show

   A. the clues of one puzzle

   B. the clues of two puzzles

   C. the paper of one wife

   D. the paper of more than one wife

3. Tell the meaning of the suffix in each word.

   ○ **American**   ○ **earthen**   ○ **lifelike**

4. In a piece of literature, the discrepancy between what appears to be true and what really is true is

   ○ metaphor   ○ irony   ○ assonance

   ○ hyperbole   ○ pun   ○ imagery

Stop the presses!

I've got a scoop!

5. Write a headline for the article.

_____

The world's largest crossword puzzle was recently unveiled. This gigantic puzzle contains 82,951 squares and a total of 12,489 clues. So far, there have been no estimates of the time it would take to complete the record-setting crossword puzzle. In any case, this a long way from the first crossword puzzle, published in 1913.

1. What does **garrulous** mean?

   The garrulous nature of the reporter charmed her editor.

2. Does the example use a semicolon properly?

   Please hand me the newspaper; it's on the coffee table.

3. Circle the prepositional phrase.

   The newspaper reporter is so sneaky that he writes his column under a pseudonym.

4. Which reference source would you use to find out who said this:

   "It's not over till it's over."

5. Which word is the most precise choice for the context?

   When Alexander decided to read the comic section of a newspaper in class, the history teacher gave him a harsh _____ .

   a. oration   c. talk

   b. response   d. admonishment

Read all about it.

Name

Read

1. What is different about this crossword puzzle?
2. What is the theme of the puzzle?
3. Find three words in the puzzle that could be verbs.
4. Find a word that could be a noun or a verb.
5. Find a word that has two or more meanings.
   Tell two of the meanings.

I haven't got a clue.

Clues:

Across:

2. _____

7. _____

10. _____

12. _____

18. _____

19. _____

20. _____

21. _____

Down:

2. _____

3. _____

4. _____

5. _____

8. _____

13. _____

15. _____

23. _____

These are some of my favorite words.

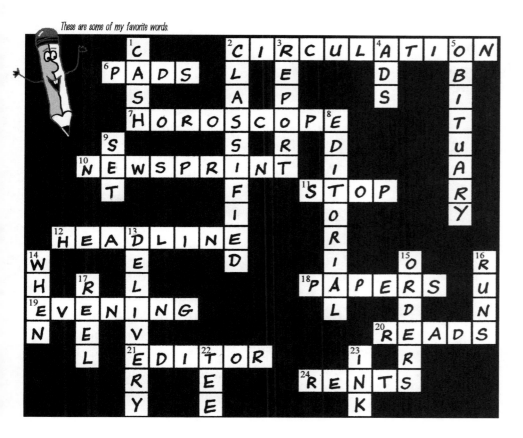

Write

This puzzle has the answers, but is missing the clues. Write the clue for each word that has a number on the clue list. Do your best to make each clue relate to the theme of the puzzle. (Some words are not included on the clue list.)

1. Sue uses these words when describing the wakeboard tricks. Spell them correctly.

exemplery   ecxiting   exquiset

extremly   exeptional   excotic

2. What does the underlined word mean?

While ice climbing, Jolene <u>exacerbated</u> her shoulder injury.

3. Circle the subordinate clause in each example.

A. Since we were running out of air, we gave up on our search for the cave.

B. It was essential that we get back to the surface quickly.

C. Everyone returned safely because we started our assent in time to avoid danger.

4. In example 5, what bias does the author show?

5. What is the main idea of the passage?

What a crazy idea! People actually fix up wheelbarrows with headlights and taillights. Then they race with them! This is not just any short little afternoon race, either. They race 100 kilometers. They race all weekend, pushing wheelbarrows along the long, varied terrain through city streets and along country highways. Who would want to do such a strange thing?

Beep, beep.

1. Write a synonym for **altercation**.

2. Does the sentence show correct pronoun usage?

Who wants to come to the guinea pig races with her and me?

3. Add correct ending punctuation.

What an exciting finish to the lizard race

Hmmm.

4. Which information can be found in a world almanac?

○ results of the latest Olympic games

○ recent population statistics for a country

○ names of leaders of world countries

○ current weather forecasts around the world

5. Rewrite the passage to include more interesting, colorful, active, or precise words or phrases. Pay special attention to replacing the underlined words.

Now here's an <u>unusual</u> recreational activity: a <u>person</u> is on a bed of sharp nails at the same time concrete blocks are <u>broken</u> on his chest. The 21 blocks <u>had</u> a total of 692 pounds of weight. Others used 16-pound sledgehammers to <u>break</u> the blocks while Chad Netherland <u>lay</u> on the blocks.

1. Add correct punctuation and capitalization.

Let's race our camel at the Geelong Camel cup Carnival Sam suggested to Sara we could win a thousand dollars

2. Finish the analogy.

noisy : clamorous :: _____ : superb

○ raucous   ○ clamor
○ subtle   ○ splendid

3. Circle the interjection.

Oh, no! Our camel is racing the wrong way!

4. Replace the verbs with words that are more specific and interesting.

At the Millthorpe Murphy Marathon, racers carry 50 kg of potatoes as they run 1610 meters.

5. Find the pun in each example.

A. Jude cracked his shin in the egg-throwing competition.

B. I hear you're a shoe-in to win the boot-throwing contest.

C. If you're trying to win a cow-riding race, the most important thing is to keep moo-ving.

D. Count deDough is the judge for the contests at the Penny Collecting Festival.

E. All eyes are on the winner at the Potato Carnival, because she is wearing such an appealing outfit.

1. Give the two different meanings of the two homographs in the sentence.

Abigail went to the judges to contest the results of the contest.

2. What kind of phrase is underlined?

The object is <u>to toss the egg without breaking it.</u>

3. Correct any misspelled words.

A riegning beauty queen and her decietful, concieted nieghbor teamed up to compete in the local egg-throwing contest.

4. Al has borrowed a book on extreme sports. He wants to find the definitions of the ice-climbing terms used in the book. Where (in the book) should he look?

5. Revise the passage to make it flow more smoothly, and to give it more variety in sentence length and structure.

Some people race lizards. They get together in Eulo, Queensland. They go to a race track that is specially built, built just for racing lizards. They take their lizards along. The event begins with a lizard auction. Then they race their lizards in five different events. They can win prizes if their lizard wins a race.

Use It! Don't Lose It! IP 612-3

Read

I'm bugged.

1. Identify the mode of this selection (expository, narrative, imaginary, persuasive, or personal-expressive).
2. Circle an inference made by the author of this selection.
3. What is the difference between Katie's winning spitting distance and the world record?
4. Which event at the Bug Bowl would you most like to watch (or NOT watch)?
5. What precaution does a cricket spitter need to take when getting ready to spit the insect?

Imagine putting a dead bug on your tongue—not just once, but many times a day. "Why," you wonder, "would anyone do that?" Just ask teenager Katie Herrnstein, cricket-spitting competitor at Purdue University's 1998 Annual Bug Bowl. Katie won the competition for the second year in a row to become the Junior World's Champion. She spit a cricket 16 feet, 2 inches to win this title. The honor received so much attention that Katie was invited to fly to Paris to show her cricket-spitting skills on French television.

Another cricket-spitting champion is even better known for this unusual talent. Danny Capps of Wisconsin holds the world record (as certified for the Guinness World Records). He spit a cricket 30 feet, 1.2 inches to set a new record. Like Katie, Danny has had a long interest in insects, and is not the least bit bothered by the practice of holding dead bugs on the tongue.

How does someone spit a cricket far enough to win a competition or set a record? According to Katie Herrnstein, you place the cricket (dead, of course) in the center of your tongue near the front. Then you take a deep breath, being careful not to swallow the insect. Finally, you exhale as hard as you can—just as if you were spitting a watermelon seed or a spitball.

Cricket spitting is just one of the insect activities that draws visitors to Purdue University every April. Thousands of people also pet insects in a petting zoo, watch cockroach races, enjoy many insect exhibits, and taste foods cooked with insects or honey. The popularity of these events shows that many people beyond Katie and Danny are comfortable with bugs.

Write

Create a brief "How-To" manual that teaches the reader how to do some unusual sport or activity. For example, explain how to. . .

win a bathtub race

train a slug to race

train a lizard to do tricks

throw and catch an egg without breaking it

toss a boot a winning distance

win a bubble-blowing contest

eat 20 doughnuts in one minute

peel a banana in record time

Faster!

1. What punctuation should go in the blank?

○ parentheses   ○ colon
○ ellipsis   ○ semicolon

"I'd like to loan you my tent," said Will, "but the last time you borrowed it _____ remember what happened?"

2. The part of the story that tells about the campers' escape from the bear and safe journey home is probably the story's

○ resolution   ○ exposition
○ setting   ○ climax

3. What is the connotation of **campfire**?

4. Identify a cause and an effect.

George's terrible blisters are the price he's paying for not breaking in the new hiking boots before the camping trip.

5. Identify each sentence as D (declarative), IN (interrogative), IM (imperative), or E (exclamatory)

____ A. Did you bring bear repellant?

____ B. I forgot the freeze dried food.

____ C. Swat that mosquito, please.

____ D. Look out for the poison ivy!

____ E. Don't touch that plant!

____ F. Paddle the canoe that way.

I'm getting quite a workout.

1. Correct the misspelled words.

Lulu brout chocalate, mosquitoe repellaint, and a fishing lisence along on the hike.

Buzz!

Buzz!

2. What is the meaning of the root that these words have in common?

formula   reform   conform

formulate formation   deformity

3. Eliminate excess words.

The hikers they totally and completely panicked at the sight of the bear they just saw along the trail.

What's all the buzz?

4. What reference book is a collection of articles telling about the lives of people and their accomplishments, arranged alphabetically?

5. Write the correct pronouns in each blank. Some words may be used twice.

interrogative _____

possessive _____

intensive _____

demonstrative _____

indefinite _____

reflexive _____

whose   mine   yours

myself   that   it

this   which   everybody

1. Add correct punctuation and capitalization.

who was it that asked do you hear a bear breathing heavily outside this tent

2. Circle the appositive.

I found something we need, dry firewood.

3. Find a pair of homonyms to complete each sentence.

A. On the hike up the mountain, did you get a

_____ at the _____?
(look)   (apex)

B. I don't want to see that _____
(animal)
_____ his teeth at me.
(expose)

4. Which sign in 5 shows **alliteration**?

5. Give a general summarizing statement about what the signs are saying.

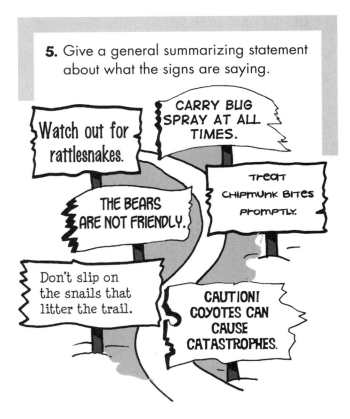

Watch out for rattlesnakes.

CARRY BUG SPRAY AT ALL TIMES.

THE BEARS ARE NOT FRIENDLY.

TREAT CHIPMUNK BITES PROMPTLY.

Don't slip on the snails that litter the trail.

CAUTION! COYOTES CAN CAUSE CATASTROPHES.

1. Which word does not fit into the same classification as the others?

○ rascal   ○ ransack   ○ rattle
○ ramble   ○ rankle   ○ ratify

2. Correct this sentence.

I could of brought marshmallows if you would of told me you needed them.

3. Which words are spelled correctly?

○ parenthetical   ○ peculierly
○ simultaneously   ○ orthadontist

4. Would information about the Pacific Crest Hiking Trail be found on an encyclopedia page with the guide words **penicillin** and **Pyrenees Mountains**?

5. Rewrite this poem as prose.

A campground's full of dirty stuff.
The campfire adds more grit.
Sooty pots and grimy pans—
You can't get away from it!
It's all around the campsite
Dust here, grime everywhere
On your skin, inside your bags
On everything you use and wear.
If you're going to be a camper
Forget that nice clean shirt
Make friends with dust, and grime, and soot
Just get used to all the dirt.

Read

1. Which example uses onomatopoeia?
2. Circle two examples of personification.
3. Identify a phrase that is effective in creating suspense.
4. What image is created by example 2?
5. To which sense or senses does example 3 appeal?

Every campfire needs a ghost story.

A Ghostly Quartet

1 We were telling jokes around the campfire, never dreaming what was lurking out just beyond the rim of light from the fire. It was not until the fired died down that the dreadful rasping, gasping, choke . . . choke . . . choke echoed through the campsite.

2 The wind howled like a wounded animal and shook the tent with angry claws. Three terrified campers huddled inside, slightly consoled by the faint glimmer from the last flashlight.

4 The girls should have made it to the campsite before dark, but the wind's strong arms pushed against their canoe, and the paddling was slow. Just at dusk, they were nearing shore. Just at dusk, something was waiting for them at the campsite—something they had never seen before.

3 "Stop that moaning," snapped Jack. "It isn't funny!"

"I'm not moaning," Tom replied.

"Well, who is?" Tom and Jack looked at each other, suddenly realizing that the sound was not coming from inside the tent. Just at that moment, the zipper of the tent began an upward slide—without the help of either boy. A hand slithered its way through the open slit.

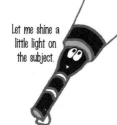

Let me shine a little light on the subject.

Write

Choose two of the ghost stories to finish. Choose words and phrases that will accomplish the purpose of making the listeners tremble. Pay special attention to the ending of your story. You will want the listeners to be very apprehensive!

1. What is the correct punctuation to place after the greeting in a business letter?

2. Tell the part of speech of each underlined word in the sentence.

   A person can <u>survive</u> as long as <u>twelve</u> days <u>without</u> water if the temperature is not <u>higher</u> than 70° F.

3. What is a **charlatan**?

4. What literary technique is shown with the use of the words **drip, drip, drip** and **kerplunk**?

   Adrift in the raft, he was awakened by the drip, drip, drip of rainwater on the rim of his hat and the kerplunk of fish jumping just beyond his feet.

I'm drifting.

5. Why would the solar still be an important factor in the Steven Callahan's survival?

   In January 1982, a man named Steven Callahan set sail for a trip on a boat he had built. After six days at sea, the boat sank and he was left with only an inflatable raft. He had a little food, some water, and a solar still for removing salt from seawater. Steven was able to stay alive for 76 days, even though his raft sprung leaks. He drifted 1800 miles in the raft before he was rescued. Steven believes that the solar still was a major factor in his survival.

1. Find a synonym for **fracas**.

2. Peyton spent four days wandering around the woods trying to find his way back to the campsite. Did he **loose** or **lose** his way?

3. Is the verb **transitive** or **intransitive**?

   During his time adrift on the sea, Steve Callahan fought off sharks.

I've never been lost in the woods.

4. Choose the most precise word to complete the sentence below.

   To conserve food the marooned sailors _____ each morsel slowly.

   ○ devoured   ○ ate   ○ nibbled
   ○ tasted   ○ licked   ○ savored

5. How many February days did not have a shark-sighting?

   Jan 8 – set sail from St. Croix

   Jan 14 – boat sank

   Jan 30 – ran out of food

   Feb 4 – saw 3 sharks

   Feb 7 – saw 1 shark

   Feb 11 – saw 2 sharks

   Feb 16 – raft sprung a leak

   Feb 19 – saw 6 sharks

   Feb 29 – saw 2 sharks

   Mar 1 – got rescued

1. What word could be combined with each of these to form a compound word?

○ arrow   ○ light   ○ line
○ egg   ○ band   ○ letter

2. Add **-ing** and **-ed** to each word.

monkey   worry   muddy

3. Which examples are correct?

a. Bethany is the swimmer who survived.

b. Was it Bethany whom survived the attack?

c. Who is it that was attacked?

d. Was it the same shark whom attacked Greg?

4. Choose the correct literary device.

The surfers were tossed like rag dolls, tumbling in a frothy mixture of foam and seaweed.

○ simile   ○ hyperbole
○ alliteration ○ pun

I'm always alert for people adrift.

5. Circle the effect in each example.

a. She was rescued after she waved down a passing ship.

b. The skier got lost because of the blinding blizzard.

c. Steven was able to drink pure water because he had a solar still.

d. When the elevator cable was severed, the elevator car fell 75 stories.

e. Someone locked the door early, leaving Bev stuck in the store overnight.

1. Which words need capital letters?

former olympic hockey player eric lemarque got lost on his snowboard and survived seven days in califorina's sierra nevada mountains.

2. Circle antonyms for **survive**.

succumb   subsist   persist

endure   perish   resist

3. Edit this sentence.

On july 28 1945 Betty lou oliver survive a 1000 foot fall in an elevator at the empire state building in new york city new york

4. Alphabetize these words.

survive   survival   surrender

surplice   surplus   surreptitious

Everyone needs a crutch sometimes.

5. Tell what should be changed to correct the usage in each example.

a. It is well that you survived the fall.

b. I'm surely she was lost 10 days.

c. He fell very quick after Jim.

d. The surfers were real scared of the sharks.

e. Should you lay down when you meet a cougar?

f. I think you should have risen up your arms when you met the bear.

g. That grizzly behaved bad when I met him on the trail.

Read

1. What is the theme of these selections?

2. Circle an opinion in one of the selections.

3. Circle a fact in one of the selections.

4. Which ordeal lasted the longest?

5. Tell which ordeal you think would be the hardest one to survive (and why).

(2003) Bethany Hamilton, a 15-year old surfer, survived a shark attack in the waters off a beach in Hawaii.

(1972) An unnamed cat survived eight days, trapped in the rubble of a building that collapsed during an earthquake.

(1942) Poom Lim survived 133 days along on a raft adrift in the Atlantic Ocean.

(1945) Betty Lou Oliver survived an amazing plunge in an elevator. An elevator in the Empire State Building fell 75 stories when its cables were severed. Ms. Oliver was inside that elevator and lived to tell about it.

(1988) Kively Popa John survived six days trapped in an elevator. Fortunately, she had just been to the market and had a bag of fruit, vegetables, and bread along with her.

(1986) A two-year old girl, Michelle Funk, survived 66 minutes underwater in a creek. She made a full recovery after her rescue.

(1972) Vesna Vulovic fell 33,333 feet inside a section of an aircraft. She is the survivor of the longest fall (without a parachute) on record.

(1954-1994) Charles Jensen endured 970 surgeries.

I'd better stand by, I might be needed.

Write

1. Write a title for this group of selections.

2. Write three questions you would like to ask each survivor.

1. Give correct capitalization to the book's cover.

I love to read

the last ball game

by claus d. park

2. Circle the complete predicate.

Mario skidded about half the distance between the two bases.

3. What is the meaning of the underlined word?

It was a <u>daunting</u> task to try to get a strike out of Spike Malone. The pitcher tried again and again, and just couldn't do it.

4. Choose the correct literary device.

In the game today, Lucy was a tiger every time she got up to bat.

○ personification   ○ irony
○ simile   ○ metaphor

5. Number the events in a reasonable sequence.

____ The next time up to bat, she struck out.

____ Maria slid to first.

____ Then she got two strikes in a row.

____ It was Maria's first turn to bat.

____ Maria passed third base on her way to home plate.

____ The first two pitches were balls.

____ She hit the ball past third base.

____ On Jana's hit, she stole second.

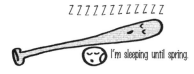

ZZZZZZZZZZZZZ

I'm sleeping until spring.

1. Correct the usage error in the sentence.

How come you didn't stop at second base?

2. Circle the correctly spelled words.

citazen   oppisit   occurence

advertize   busness   arithmatic

3. Finish the analogy.

blush : embarrassment :: fume : _____

4. Which key word should you use to find information about famous hitters (such as Babe Ruth) in baseball history?

○ history   ○ Babe Ruth   ○ players
○ hitters   ○ major league ○ baseball

5. Rewrite the sentences to make the sentences more interesting and the verbs more active.

a. **The umpire said, "Strike three!" as the ball whipped past the batter's head.**

b. **Running around the bases, Ramon looked like a streaking meteor.**

c. **The wind at the ballpark was piercing.**

Take me out to the ball game.

Use It! Don't Lose It! IP 612-3

1. The enthusiasm for the winning team is spreading. Is the enthusiasm **contagious** or **infectious**?

2. Insert apostrophes correctly.

Youve got to remember that its only Toms first time at bat in his whole life.

3. What literary technique is used here?

Thick sheets of silver rain separated the fans from the field.

4. Circle and identify the verbal in each sentence (gerund, infinitive, or participle).

   a. Screaming made my throat sore.

   b. The screaming fans waved banners.

   c. Jim was the last one to scream.

   d. Fans screaming at the top of their lungs drove me away from the ballpark.

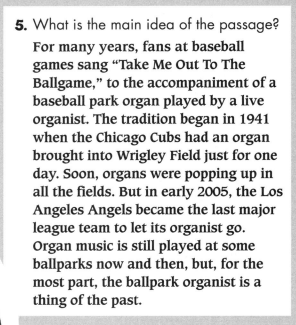

Whack!

5. What is the main idea of the passage?

For many years, fans at baseball games sang "Take Me Out To The Ballgame," to the accompaniment of a baseball park organ played by a live organist. The tradition began in 1941 when the Chicago Cubs had an organ brought into Wrigley Field just for one day. Soon, organs were popping up in all the fields. But in early 2005, the Los Angeles Angels became the last major league team to let its organist go. Organ music is still played at some ballparks now and then, but, for the most part, the ballpark organist is a thing of the past.

 It's a home run.

1. Explain the meaning of **gaffe**.

Fans said the player made a gaffe.

2. Circle the direct object(s).

The same man who invented baseball fired the first shot for the Union in the American Civil War.

3. Could a tale about a baseball game played in the 25th century be a nonfiction book?

   ○ yes   ○ no

4. Correct the spelling.

   thesuarus   **beerd**

   coogar   **drowght**

   angwish   **bosterous**

5. Write a caption for the picture.

Read

1. What is the point of view in this poem?
2. Give a brief oral or written summary. Tell what the author is trying to say.
3. Describe what you believe the poet really feels about the broken window.
4. Make an inference about the relationship between the baseball player and the person who is receiving the apology.

I Need To Tell You...

The baseball has broken your dining room window
And I know company's coming for dinner
Forgive me
It was a fine hit
And I got a home run.

Uh oh.

Write

Have you ever apologized for something for which you were not truly sorry? Think about it. Make a list of such events (real or imaginary). Then follow the form of the poem above to write an apology poem. (Look in your library or on the Internet for a copy of the poem *This is Just to Say* by poet William Carlos Williams. This poem was modeled after Mr. Williams' famous apology poem.)

Title _____

Line 1
What I did _____

Line 2
Why it's a problem _____

Line 3
Some words or phrases
that give the apology _____

Lines 4-5
A hint as to why you
are not truly sorry _____

_____

1. Circle the words that are spelled correctly.

○ attendence   ○ abundance   ○ consequence
○ assurance   ○ nuisance   ○ transferance

2. Write a synonym for **paucity**.

3. For each example, tell if the verb is an **action** verb or a **linking** verb.

   a. The Sears Tower looms above other buildings in Chicago.

   b. Elevators rise at 1,600 feet a minute.

   c. The tower's cost was over $150 million.

4. What literary technique is shown here?
The traffic light winked its yellow eye at me.

5. Read each title and make an inference about what you might find in the book.

If Traffic Lights Could Talk

How Traffic Lights Work

The Traffic Light That Changed My Life

The Day The Traffic Lights Refused To Change

1. The city's mayor warned people about the discovery of noxious substances. What does she mean by **noxious**?

It's a crowded world.

2. Does the sentence show correct use of parentheses?

The city of Seoul (South Korea's capital) has a population greater than that of Australia.

3. Rewrite this to clarify the meaning.

I learned that the population of Sao Paulo, Brazil increases by 2,000 people a day from reading an almanac.

4. Think of five words that could be found on a glossary page with the guide words **causeway** and **city**.

5. Edit the passage for punctuation, capitalization, and spelling.

Middletown Connecticut is a small city of 45000 people situated in a pleasent spot along the connecticut river. In resent years the city is growing and becoming a particulerly attractive setting for new busnesses. Thirty five busnesses have opened in a downtown mall called the main street market, other additions are two new Golf Corses and a new 12-screen movie theater complex.

110

1. What is the meaning of this sentence?

Todd and his friend were on top of the world because they won a trip to Paris.

2. Circle the silent letters.

**an honest ghost
a whimpering gnome
a psychic knight
a gourmet wrestler**

3. Does the subject agree with the verb?

San Francisco, my favorite of all cities, have many beautiful bridges.

4. True or false?

Expository writing is writing that informs, teaches, or explains.

5. Compare the two lists. What do you notice about the similarities and differences?

Most Common U.S. City Names

1. Fairview
2. Midway
3. Oak Grove
4. Franklin and Riverside
5. Centerville
6. Mount Pleasant
7. Georgetown
8. Salem

Most Common U.S. Place Names

1. Fairview
2. Midway
3. Riverside
4. Oak Grove
5. Five Points
6. Oakland
7. Greenwood
8. Bethel and Franklin
(Includes cities and other places such as parks, airports, etc.)

I should know this!

1. Give the meaning of each root.

| lunar | mortal | dissect |
| portable | dynamite | dormant |

2. Capitalize and punctuate the sentence.

Venice a city in italy has the distinction of being the worlds most waterlogged city

3. What reference source is an alphabetical list of items or information, found in a book, magazine, or set of publications?

4. Is the underlined clause an essential clause?

Las Vegas, <u>a city set in the desert of Nevada,</u> is the wedding capital of the world.

5. Eliminate unnecessary words.

The city of Liverpool, England, a city in England, is famous for the number of musicians who call it home. There have been more number one top of the chart hit singles by people from Liverpool, in relation to the number of people in the population, than from any other city in the world.

Interesting.

Read

Examine this picture of the "goings-on" in the apartments and stores on this city street.

1. Make an inference about each scenario (A–H). Tell what you think is happening.

2. Predict what will happen next in two of the settings.

Write

1. Write a creative title for a story about window F.

2. Write an inviting beginning for a description of the happenings in window D.

3. Write part of a conversation that is going on in window G.

4. Write a question you would like to ask one the persons in window E.

5. Write a smashing ending for a story about window A.

INCENTIVE PUBLICATIONS DAILY PRACTICE SERIES
GRADE 8 LANGUAGE SKILLS

Vocabulary & Word Skills

Skill	1	2	3	4	5	6	7	8	9	10	11	12	13	14	15	16	17	18	19	20	21	22	23	24	25	26	27	28	29	30	31	32	33	34	35	36
Prefix, suffix, and root meanings	√		√			√			√			√		√	√	√		√			√	√			√		√	√		√	√		√			√
Compound words					√			√			√						√						√			√					√			√		
Knowledge of word meanings	√			√		√	√			√	√	√	√		√	√	√	√	√	√	√	√	√			√		√				√		√	√	√
Word and phrase meaning from context	√					√		√		√				√				√	√						√			√	√						√	
Denotation and connotation		√						√														√							√							
Identify synonyms	√				√		√		√		√		√			√	√			√	√				√	√		√		√	√	√				√
Identify antonyms	√				√		√	√		√				√	√	√	√				√	√					√				√					
Words with similar meanings or sounds			√		√				√		√					√						√			√	√	√	√		√					√	
Homonyms				√			√												√				√		√	√		√			√	√	√			
Multiple Meanings					√		√			√	√		√		√			√		√	√					√	√		√	√	√	√				√
Meanings of figurative language			√								√		√						√					√				√	√				√		√	
Word classification		√	√														√		√	√																
Analogies		√		√			√						√	√		√		√	√			√		√			√					√		√		

Reading Comprehension

Skill	1	2	3	4	5	6	7	8	9	10	11	12	13	14	15	16	17	18	19	20	21	22	23	24	25	26	27	28	29	30	31	32	33	34	35	36
Main ideas	√	√			√			√	√		√			√	√	√		√	√	√		√				√	√	√	√	√	√	√			√	√
Supporting details			√	√	√	√		√	√		√	√	√	√	√	√		√	√	√	√	√	√	√	√	√	√	√	√	√	√		√	√		√
Sequence	√				√						√	√				√						√	√					√		√						√
Read titles, headlines, captions		√				√				√										√		√		√				√		√					√	√
Follow directions			√						√					√							√			√					√		√					
Find information	√	√		√	√			√			√	√	√	√	√	√	√	√	√	√		√		√	√	√		√	√	√				√		√
Fact and opinion	√				√							√								√				√	√				√			√		√		
Cause and effect			√			√																			√		√									√
Interpret graphs, tables, illustrations, graphics	√	√	√	√	√	√		√	√		√	√	√	√		√	√	√	√	√		√			√			√	√		√	√				√
Draw conclusions			√	√	√	√														√	√					√	√	√	√	√			√			
Make inferences		√	√	√		√	√	√	√	√		√					√					√					√	√			√			√		√
Make predictions																									√								√		√	
Compare and contrast				√				√		√		√		√	√			√		√				√		√				√	√	√		√		
Summarize																																√	√		√	
Evaluate	√	√		√	√				√			√	√	√	√	√	√	√	√	√	√	√	√	√			√	√	√	√		√	√	√		√

113

INCENTIVE PUBLICATIONS DAILY PRACTICE SERIES
GRADE 8 LANGUAGE SKILLS

Literature

Skill	1	2	3	4	5	6	7	8	9	10	11	12	13	14	15	16	17	18	19	20	21	22	23	24	25	26	27	28	29	30	31	32	33	34	35	36
Identify setting, plot, characters, theme, tone, mood, point of view	✓		✓	✓	✓					✓	✓		✓	✓		✓		✓	✓	✓	✓		✓	✓			✓			✓	✓	✓	✓	✓		
Identify writing genres and modes	✓	✓			✓		✓		✓		✓					✓		✓	✓			✓			✓	✓		✓								✓
Identify literary devices: *simile, metaphor, alliteration, puns, rhyme, rhythm, repetition, imagery, hyperbole, idioms, onomatopoeia, personification*	✓			✓		✓			✓					✓			✓							✓			✓			✓			✓		✓	✓
Identify stereotypes and bias			✓								✓	✓										✓			✓				✓			✓				
Identify author's audience and purpose			✓	✓			✓				✓				✓										✓		✓		✓							
Identify rhyming patterns of poems	✓						✓	✓									✓					✓							✓							
Identify writing techniques	✓				✓	✓			✓	✓	✓	✓	✓				✓	✓	✓			✓			✓					✓	✓	✓	✓		✓	

Writing

Skill	1	2	3	4	5	6	7	8	9	10	11	12	13	14	15	16	17	18	19	20	21	22	23	24	25	26	27	28	29	30	31	32	33	34	35	36
Choose effective words	✓		✓	✓							✓						✓				✓	✓	✓			✓		✓	✓		✓	✓	✓	✓	✓	✓
Eliminate repetitive or unnecessary words or phrases	✓				✓								✓											✓			✓			✓						✓
Write in different genres and modes	✓		✓	✓		✓	✓	✓	✓	✓	✓	✓	✓	✓	✓	✓				✓	✓	✓		✓		✓	✓	✓	✓		✓	✓	✓		✓	✓
Write prose and poetry	✓		✓					✓		✓	✓		✓	✓	✓	✓				✓	✓	✓				✓	✓	✓	✓			✓				
Write topic sentences		✓						✓				✓				✓			✓				✓				✓				✓	✓				
Add supporting details				✓		✓			✓				✓							✓	✓				✓					✓			✓		✓	
Write strong beginnings, endings							✓				✓									✓		✓				✓				✓				✓		
Write effective titles, captions, headlines	✓									✓							✓					✓					✓		✓							
Summarize a written piece				✓	✓				✓					✓				✓						✓		✓			✓	✓	✓		✓		✓	
Respond to a written piece					✓						✓	✓	✓	✓			✓		✓		✓	✓	✓	✓	✓		✓	✓	✓		✓			✓		✓
Revise for clarity, word choice, effectiveness, sequence, flow		✓					✓			✓					✓		✓	✓	✓	✓	✓			✓	✓						✓	✓		✓		
Edit sentences for spelling, usage, punctuation & capitalization	✓		✓	✓					✓	✓			✓	✓	✓	✓	✓	✓	✓	✓	✓	✓		✓	✓		✓	✓	✓	✓		✓	✓	✓	✓	✓

INCENTIVE PUBLICATIONS DAILY PRACTICE SERIES
GRADE 8 LANGUAGE SKILLS

Grammar

Skill	1	2	3	4	5	6	7	8	9	10	11	12	13	14	15	16	17	18	19	20	21	22	23	24	25	26	27	28	29	30	31	32	33	34	35	36
Sentences (completeness, kinds: complexity, purpose)	√	√										√					√			√							√		√			√			√	
Subjects & predicates	√														√	√						√	√													
Predicate nouns and adjectives	√			√				√												√					√			√				√				
Conjunctions & interjections				√														√	√													√				
Parts of speech		√	√	√	√	√	√	√							√	√	√	√	√		√		√	√						√			√			
Common, proper nouns		√	√									√		√			√	√		√			√				√									
Singular, plural nouns			√	√		√		√				√											√	√			√									
Possessive nouns			√			√		√		√				√										√							√					
Kinds of pronouns		√		√				√			√									√			√								√	√				
Verb tenses (regular, irregular)			√		√				√		√				√						√				√	√					√	√		√		
Case: nominative, objective						√		√	√		√	√						√		√			√			√				√						
Action and linking verbs						√									√	√				√						√			√							
Transitive and intransitive verbs							√						√						√											√						
Verbals (participles, infinitives, gerunds)																		√										√							√	
Comparative and superlative adjectives, adverbs					√										√									√												
Direct and indirect objects						√														√								√							√	
Prepositions; prepositional phrases						√						√						√	√												√					
Phrases: participial, gerund, infinitive									√				√					√			√	√			√							√				
Appositives							√										√												√							
Misplaced modifiers	√									√										√			√													
Different kinds of clauses (noun, adjective, adverb, independent, subordinate, essential, nonessential)										√			√		√						√	√	√						√		√	√		√		√

©2006 Incentive Publications, Inc., Nashville, TN

Use It! Don't Lose It! IP 612-3

Usage

Skill	1	2	3	4	5	6	7	8	9	10	11	12	13	14	15	16	17	18	19	20	21	22	23	24	25	26	27	28	29	30	31	32	33	34	35	36
Subject-verb agreement			✓		✓					✓																	✓									✓
Pronoun-antecedent agreement				✓			✓						✓			✓		✓													✓					
Use of *who, whom, whoever,* and *whomever*	✓				✓						✓																								✓	
Use of *who's* and *whose*		✓																✓								✓									✓	
Subject and object pronoun use				✓		✓			✓			✓									✓				✓	✓						✓				
Use of negatives					✓												✓						✓							✓						
Usage of adjectives-adverbs that are easily confused			✓											✓	✓														✓							
Other usage: double subjects, use of *have* as verb								✓							✓							✓		✓										✓		✓

Capitalization & Punctuation

Skill	1	2	3	4	5	6	7	8	9	10	11	12	13	14	15	16	17	18	19	20	21	22	23	24	25	26	27	28	29	30	31	32	33	34	35	36
Capitalization of proper nouns and adjectives	✓			✓					✓						✓			✓		✓		✓		✓	✓			✓		✓		✓	✓	✓	✓	
Capitalization in titles			✓									✓				✓						✓		✓					✓					✓	✓	
Commas		✓						✓		✓					✓	✓	✓	✓		✓	✓	✓	✓		✓	✓	✓	✓		✓	✓	✓	✓			✓
Ending punctuation	✓									✓		✓			✓	✓	✓	✓		✓	✓	✓			✓	✓		✓	✓	✓			✓			
Colons, semicolons			✓			✓			✓														✓							✓						
Quotation marks				✓		✓							✓	✓					✓		✓						✓									
Hyphens, dashes, parentheses, and ellipses				✓	✓		✓				✓						✓	✓				✓		✓												✓
Apostrophes			✓		✓			✓		✓		✓			✓		✓			✓	✓	✓		✓	✓				✓		✓			✓		✓
Capitalization and punctuation in sentences and titles	✓			✓		✓							✓						✓																	✓
Capitalization and punctuation in quotations								✓								✓										✓								✓		
Capitalization and punctuation in letters					✓																	✓												✓		

INCENTIVE PUBLICATIONS DAILY PRACTICE SERIES
GRADE 8 LANGUAGE SKILLS

Spelling

Skill	1	2	3	4	5	6	7	8	9	10	11	12	13	14	15	16	17	18	19	20	21	22	23	24	25	26	27	28	29	30	31	32	33	34	35	36
Words with ie	√												√					√							√								√			
Confusing consonant and vowel spellings							√			√																								√		
Singular and plural nouns				√	√							√		√						√				√		√						√				
Past tense of verbs			√	√	√				√			√										√						√								
Words with silent letters						√		√				√											√						√	√						
Words with final y							√		√					√													√									
Words that end in o				√												√																				
Correct spelling of endings			√			√							√	√				√						√												
Confusing words						√			√						√																√		√			
Identify correctly spelled words	√		√		√	√								√		√						√										√		√		
Correct misspelled words		√	√	√				√							√	√					√									√	√				√	
Spell words correctly		√	√	√				√		√				√	√	√	√		√	√			√	√					√		√	√	√	√	√	√

Study & Research Skills

Skill	1	2	3	4	5	6	7	8	9	10	11	12	13	14	15	16	17	18	19	20	21	22	23	24	25	26	27	28	29	30	31	32	33	34	35	36
Alphabetical order	√									√			√								√						√							√		
Guide words		√				√	√		√				√					√			√	√						√					√		√	
Key words			√								√					√	√	√								√										√
Dictionary, encyclopedia entries			√		√	√		√	√		√	√		√	√	√	√			√		√	√			√		√	√				√		√	√
Purposes and uses of different reference materials			√					√				√		√	√			√					√						√		√					
Parts of a book	√					√									√				√			√					√			√			√			√
Information from a map, illustration, diagram, other graphics		√					√													√		√								√				√	√	
Information from tables, charts, timelines, outlines				√	√					√			√			√								√	√				√	√	√			√		
Fiction, biography, non-fiction				√					√					√				√			√			√				√				√			√	
Library organization			√	√							√						√	√																		

117

©2006 Incentive Publications, Inc., Nashville, TN

Use It! Don't Lose It! IP 612-3

ANSWER KEY

Week 1 (pages 5–7)

MONDAY
1. National, Football, League, Walter, Payton, Chicago, Bears
2. plot
3. a, im, non, in, dis, il, un
4. b
5. b, c

TUESDAY
1. adjective
2. irate
3. 1 score, 2 scoreboard, 3 scored, 4 scoring, 5 serve, 6 service
4. peeved, piqued, incensed
5. When the New York Yankees headed for California, they flew from the John F. Kennedy Airport. Did they fly over the Grand Canyon or the Rocky Mountains on their way?

WEDNESDAY
1. abab
2. reign, sleigh
3. get, obtain
4. b, c
5. By halftime, the score was tied.

THURSDAY
1. exclamation point
2. an index
3. Jackie, the player wearing number ten,
4. sad, gloomy, in a dark mood
5. In my opinion OR I think; 16-year old OR teenage; worst OR most awful; I am sorry that I spent seven dollars for the ticket OR I feel my money was wasted; Hopefully OR I wish.

FRIDAY
Read:
1. a. news article; b. joke; c. tall tale; d. explanation or short essay; e. poem; f. letter
2. Sam thinks the orange socks helped him win the tennis championship.
3. Any one of these phrases or sentences: The weather was so hot that the rubber was melting off the tennis balls; the referee's nose burst into flames; he leaped twelve feet into the air; sent the ball above the clouds; in just under 45 seconds, he had won the tournament.
4. a and d
5. Coach Stringer
Write: Titles and missing limerick lines will vary.

Week 2 (pages 8–10)

MONDAY
1. Shamu, Ocean, Beach (or Atlantic Ocean), Beach (or Agate Beach), Bridge (or Bay Bridge)
2. After swimming, we picked up shells, ate lunch, put on sunscreen, and napped on the beach.
3. Not compound: sandwich, submarine
4. no

5. Answers will vary. The author seems to dislike the beach.

TUESDAY
1. a
2. raucous, terrorize, fearsome, explosion
3. Answers will vary: I, me, my, mine, we, our, ours, us
4. 156
5. b, c

WEDNESDAY
1. a
2. wholesome
3. Twenty Thousand Leagues Under The Sea OR
Twenty Thousand Leagues Under the Sea
4. Cause: the pirate ship sank in a wild storm; Effect: the treasure ended up at the bottom of the ocean.
5. Answers may vary. The author wants to be rescued from the island.

THURSDAY
1. Answers will vary: to rush ahead, to pay for something with a credit card (buy now, pay later), an accusation, to give new life to a battery, to give an assignment to someone
2. license, escape, cafeteria, whale or wail
3. a
4. Answers will vary.
5. Answers will vary.

FRIDAY
Read:
1. 8:00 pm
2. They are very cold.
3. Answers will vary. One might conclude that the waters are cold and dangerous, or that the beach is well monitored or carefully controlled for safety.
4. yes; the signs do not prohibit picnics
Write: Answers may vary.
1. While driving a dune buggy on Lost Creek Beach, Mom whistled to her dog.
2. When we had Sam join us for lunch on the beach, Alex and I laughed a lot.
3. A storm came in while I was relaxing on my sailboat.
4. The swimmer's blue beach towel got washed away by a wave.
5. By mistake, Lucy dropped into the ocean the new goggles she had bought.
6. Todd caught fish, seasoned them with salt and pepper, and served them to the girls.
7. When we were paddling the raft to the shore, we noticed that the picnic looked inviting.
8. While I was waiting on my surfboard, a jellyfish stung me.
9. Shakira was in her bathing suit ready to go in the water when she saw a shark.
10. The water looked good to us, since we were tired and hot from running on the beach.

Week 3 (pages 11–13)

MONDAY
1. first person
2. yes
3. terrify
4. line
5. Answers may vary. Yes, it seems the author has enough information about Lee's experience with her nails to come to this conclusion.

TUESDAY
1. Answers will vary. Jonathan Friedman balanced 13 spoons on his face to set a world record.
2. flaunting
3. tunnel
4. laughter, wriggle, sure, giant, squirt
5. a. Anyway; b. beside; c. between; d. sitting

WEDNESDAY
1. Answers may vary; this is the idea: She's working too hard, or keeping long hours, or wearing herself out, or getting up early and staying up late.
2. So, my question is this: Did you know that the longest tongue in the world measures 3.7 inches and belongs to Stephen Taylor (UK)?
3. banana's peel
4. hearing
5. Answers will vary. Max is interested in extremes or record-setting events or items.

THURSDAY
1. monkeys, boxes, records, hooves, pennies, pailfuls
2. waffle (the rest begin with silent letters)
3. swam, broke, argued, leapt
4. gazetteer
5. Answers will vary.

FRIDAY
Read:
1. 3
2. 6
3. 10,711
4. 3
5. human chain
Write: Reports will vary.

Week 4 (pages 14–16)

MONDAY
1. personification
2. them, them
3. sped, caught, fought, hurried, read, loosened
4. yes
5. Answers will vary: The summary may read something like this: Fifteen holdup men and two accomplices carried out the Great Train Robbery of 1963, getting away with over two million British pounds. Many of the robbers were caught, but the money was never recovered.

TUESDAY
1. sisters-in-law, engineers, cacti, watches, teeth, knives, radios, mysteries
2. c
3. "Officer," whispered the lady in the fur coat, "that man's behavior is very suspicious."
4. sneaky, mysterious, suspicious
5. The strange man on the train platform pulled his green hat down to shield his face and turned up the collar on his long, baggy trench coat. He lingered in the shadows, furtively sneaking out and darting back to his hiding place behind a post. It wasn't long before other passengers began to notice his surreptitious behavior.

WEDNESDAY
1. Answers will vary somewhat. In general, the main idea is this: Bobbie Joe intended to rob a train but he botched the job.
2. Dr., Charles, Ryder, Pepsi Cola, Starlight, Express, Portland, Oregon
3. imperative
4. Answers may vary. silly, funny, humorous
5. Changes: clothes to close; patients to patience; bored to board; by to buy; cellar to seller; bier to beer; aloud to allowed; cot to caught; find to fined

THURSDAY
1. autobiography
2. so that
3. cellos, potato, avocado, echo, oboe, soprano
4. a
5. Answers will vary. Make sure details are fitting to the main idea of the paragraph.

FRIDAY
1. give information to train travelers to help them catch the right train to get where they want to go
2. Blythe or Tomas
3. 3 hours
4. Blythe and Tomas
5. Gulch
Write: Comparisons will vary.

Week 5 (pages 17–19)
MONDAY
1. one-half, ex-president, brother-in-law
2. exorbitance
3. a
4. opinion
5. rise, rose, risen, will rise
(or will be rising, or will have risen);
begin, began, begun, will begin
(or will be beginning, or will have begun);
grow, grew, grown, will grow
(or will be growing, or will have grown)

TUESDAY
1. advice
2. more thrilling, most thrilling
3. 1st to refuse something;·
2nd to hand something over to someone

4. Cross out triangular or that has three sides.
5. Answers will vary.

WEDNESDAY
1. waves of warm buttery popcorn-air
2. ascend, climb
3. appeal
4. Maria Ruiz
335 Court St.
Medford, OR 97504
October 7, 2005
5. The ride takes a left hairpin turn.

THURSDAY
1. Answers will vary. Some possibilities are: lighthouse, starlight; bookstore, cookbook; overtime, makeover; boardwalk, overboard
2. a
3. silliness, terrifying, justified
4. a, b, c, d
5. Answers will vary. Possible mood: panic, hurriedness, urgency; Words: raced, dashed, elbowed her way urgently, darted, tore, panted, scrambled

FRIDAY
Read:
1. Answers will vary.
2. The front seat of a roller coaster is the most thrilling place to be on the ride; The back seat of a roller coaster gives the most exciting, fastest ride.
3. Answers will vary. Each author is biased about the roller coaster position that gives the best ride.
4. Answers will vary. Discuss how students decide that phrases are facts.
5. Answers will vary. Discuss how students conclude that phrases are opinions.
6. Students might infer that the greater speed leads to greater airtime.
Write: Summaries will vary.

Week 6 (pages 20–22)
MONDAY
1. shortage
2. a, c
3. migrant, distant, negligent
4. onomatopoeia
5. mountains, canyons, forests

TUESDAY
1. no
2. hikers
3. loathe
4. Maomi Vemura was the first man to reach the North Pole alone. This Japanese explorer arrived at his goal on April 29, 1978.
5. a. 27; b. 25; c. 26; d. 28; e. 25; f. 27

WEDNESDAY
1. life
2. she was forced to forage something to eat from her natural surroundings

3. Scarcely anybody has completed the Pacific Crest Trail yet this year.
4. "Watch out for the falling rocks!" yelled Roc to the hiker behind him. Samantha hollered back, "I see them!"
5. Answers will vary. Students might mention active verbs, varied sentence length, repeated short sentences to give the idea of fright or paralysis, metaphor, imagery of the running, panting bear, suspense

THURSDAY
1. impunity
2. chocolate candy–fudge;
giggle–laugh;
apparition–ghost;
mute–dumb;
pen name–pseudonym
3. table of contents
4. preposition: along; object: trail
5. Answers will vary.
Some possibilities:
a. Joe complained miserably about his mosquito bites.
b. That bear is looming very near!
c. In confusion, Tom wanders along a trail that is probably the wrong one.
d. Don't you hear thunder rumbling?

FRIDAY
Read:
1. yes
2. Last Chance Creek, Bigfoot River, North Fork Creek
3. about two miles
4. Agate Campsite
5. northwest
Write: Check student directions to see that they are accurate.

Week 7 (pages 23–25)
MONDAY
1. foul, cymbal, carat, towed, pore, wrap
2. leisurely, neither, weird
3. they
4. Answers will vary; possible moods are: sleepy, slow, lazy, quiet
5. Answers will vary.
Similarities: both outside a vehicle, both allow people to see life below the surface, both can use a mask and wetsuit;
Differences: different depths, differences in equipment, one kind holds breath, the other does not

TUESDAY
1. The diver was very nervous.
2. Did you know that the biggest canyons in the world are under the Bering Sea off the coast of Alaska? Navarin Canyon is 60 miles wide. That's six times wider than the Grand Canyon!
3. a, c
4. water. waterlogged; watery; wetsuit, wetter, whack
5. Answers will vary.

ANSWER KEY

WEDNESDAY
1. probably not
2. After the incident with the shark (the one with the mean look on his face), Georgia was wary of scuba diving.
3. A. famous oceanographer; B. the first diver to get back to the boat; C. the skin diver with the string of freshly-caught fish
4. a–b–b–b–b–b–a–a
5. Answers will vary. The diver (author) escaped from the shark.

THURSDAY
1. honor
2. whistling, witch, chorus, chemists
3. swam
4. Answers will vary.
5. no

FRIDAY
1. In the introduction and the conclusion, the author expresses opinions that the dangers outweigh the benefits.
2. Answers will vary. Some opinions: But the thrills of this adventure are outweighed by the many risks to human life and health. As you can see, it is the most dangerous of all sports.
3. There are many facts in the passage. Answers will vary.
4. Answers will vary; to give information about the dangers of underwater diving OR to discourage people from underwater diving
5. prospective divers
Write: Beginnings will vary.

Week 8 (pages 26–28)
MONDAY
1. expository
2. Have you met Jeremy, Mark, and Carlos, the men who took the world's longest taxi ride?
3. satisfaction; a group or family
4. car
5. Because the Seiad Valley Café offers a huge stack of pancakes free to anyone who can finish it, the restaurant is labeled one of the world's best places to "pig out."

TUESDAY
1. Answers will vary: the Internet, a big city newspaper, the weather TV channel
2. abhor—revere; mediocre—exemplary
3. b
4. itineraries, chiefs, rodeos, yachts
5. Titles will vary.

WEDNESDAY
1. Cross out they
2. a
3. benefit, memorize, laboratory, although
4. Answers will vary.
5. Answers will vary. Students may argue either way.

THURSDAY
1. Ten Places I'll Never Visit Again
2. passenger, discontinued, seventeen
3. a
4. noun
5. Answers will vary.

FRIDAY
1. sends slimy hissing serpents to slink alongside
2. constricted
3. beware, care, there
4. calling your name, calling your name OR stay away Or new sights, new plights, new promises
5. There are some travel sites that should be avoided.
6. Answers will vary: Alaska's cold, Sahara's dryness, Antarctica's long, dark, cold nights
7. dentist's chair, musty basement
Write: Diary entries, topic sentences, and details will vary.

Week 9 (pages 29–31)
MONDAY
1. compliment
2. Ice sailing began in Holland, spread across Northern Europe, and became a popular Russian pastime.
3. adjectives: skillful, ice; adverb: deadly
4. a
5. Check to see if student has followed directions successfully.

TUESDAY
1. playful
2. thought, knew, spoke, laid, raised, snowed
3. traveling 50 mph
4. snowplow, skimpy, slippery
5. Answers will vary: Racing down snowy hills on snow shovels began as a way for ski lift operators to get down the hill at the end of the day, and has grown into a popular sport.

WEDNESDAY
1. colon
2. yes
3. b
4. letter telling about all the sights from a ski lift; poster telling what a missing sled dog looks like
5. Answers will vary somewhat; Pairs figure skating is beautiful but dangerous.

THURSDAY
1. de (detract)
2. Fiction tells an imaginary tale. Nonfiction is factual.
3. c
4. horrified or horrifying, monkeying, worried or worrying, silliness, loneliness, iced or icing
5. Each year thousands of people enjoy taking a Polar Bear Swim. Well, maybe they don't actually enjoy it, but they sure like bragging about it once they've done it! A Polar Bear Swim is an event where people jump into freezing cold bodies of water in the winter: lakes, rivers, or oceans. They stay in the water for only a few seconds. Polar Bear Swims are a very popular New Year's Day activity.

FRIDAY
1. breaking any one of the ski hill rules
2. green circles or blue triangles
3. not turn sharply in front of another skier, not ski in areas beyond ability level, not ski outside marked boundaries
4. Answers will vary: 4:30 or 5:00 pm
5. an indentation in the snow caused by falling
Write: Answers will vary.

Week 10 (pages 32–34)
MONDAY
1. dried out
2. scissors, Christmas, squeeze, pneumonia, giant, camel
3. had drunk
4. students studying the Sahara Desert
5. Answers will vary somewhat; Cave paintings have told us that the Sahara Desert was not always as dry as it is today.

TUESDAY
1. "Hey, everybody!" shouted the guide, "Look at this 700-foot high sand dune!"
2. Change it to they.
3. c
4. Drop the word he In the second sentence, change of to have.
5. painted desert

WEDNESDAY
1. simple subject = rainfall, simple predicate = measures
2. Answers will vary. torrid = cold or frigid; parched = damp, moist, wet; secluded = public
3. regretted, napping, truly, reddish
4. simile, personification active verbs, alliteration
5. Answers will vary: The author never really tells the reader how to climb a sand dune.

THURSDAY
1. dual—double; flee—to run away or escape from; hale—to beckon with a wave
2. one desert's temperatures; two camels' humps; three lizards' tails
3. Carla wore a red scarf to keep the sand out of her eyes when she rode on a camel. OR, When Carla rode on the camel, she wore a red scarf to keep the sand out of her eyes.
4. cache, cactus, Caesar, cahoots, Cairo, camouflage
5. Answers will vary.

FRIDAY
1. Answers will vary; mystery
2. third person
3. a desert
4. After the sandstorm stopped, the twins found they were alone.
5. Answers will vary; fierce winds, stinging sand, and blackening skies, OR a little, crooked spiral of sand scuttled past, whistling and whispering
6. Answers will vary. At the very least, the title tells the reader that the passage is about deserts.

Write: Odes will vary.

Week 11 (pages 35–37)
MONDAY
1. b
2. I really did beat Tony Hawk in a skateboarding competition—not that I could ever convince you of that.
3. Answers will vary; sandstorm, footprint, flashback, lookout
4. yes
5. a math class or school

TUESDAY
1. on his elbow
2. college
3. a
4. Answers will vary.
5. Answers will vary. Similarities: both are board-riding activities, similar tricks are done in both sports; Differences: wakeboard is narrower; wakeboard has mountings for feet; wakeboard is done on water and skateboarding is done on land

WEDNESDAY
1. The designers had to start over at the beginning.
2. a
3. acrobatic, elite, thorough, traction, dynamite, simultaneously
4. b, c
5. Answers will vary; All skateboards have essentially the same components.

THURSDAY
1. Though there are many theories on the subject, no one is certain about the origins of skateboarding.
2. her
3. defiance
4. a
5. Bias: Writer is in favor of a skateboard park. OR, Writer feels suspicious or unsupportive of the council members. Conclusion: Answers will vary. Check to see that the conclusion is a summarizing statement.

FRIDAY
1. to inform
2. skateboarders
3. road rash
4. ankle
5. narrow escape

Write: Poems will vary.

Week 12 (pages 38–40)
MONDAY
1. rhubarb – h; wrinkle – w; hymn – n; wedge – d; muscle – c; heiress – h
2. a,d
3. er, ist, or, ent
4. step-by-step account of your first sky dive
5. Answers will vary; Students might conclude that Susan is nervous about the jump.

TUESDAY
1. "The Youngest Balloonist Crosses the Continent"
2. circle On and with; underline On November 1–12, 2003 and with a parachute
3. a tight restraint that restricts blood flow to a bleeding area
4. ballooning
5. High wire walkers have entertained circus crowds for years. Sometimes the best performers would walk without a net below the wire. Now, many have taken the act outside the circus tent. Jay Cochran holds the world record for the highest and longest high wire act. He crossed the Qutang Gorge in China, 1,350 feet above the Yangtze River.

WEDNESDAY
1. scissors, valleys, bridesmaids, countries, horseflies, great-aunts
2. no
3. that some words are missing from the quote
4. Answers will vary; Author stereotypes bungee jumpers as a certain type of person who lives dangerously and wants to die
5. Answers will vary. The last two sentences have opinions.

THURSDAY
1. plunged, took, surfed, used, flew, hurried, was, brought
2. stymie
3. attendance, insurance, reliance, occurrence, acceptance, absence
4. almanac
5. Answers will vary.

FRIDAY
1. imaginative (or narrative or tall tale)
2. bungee jumping with a piano
3. Answers will vary. There are may.
4. a move as swift as a sneeze
5. Active verbs are: defied, leapt, scooped, mixed, guzzled, snapped, jumped, hurtled, wrestled

Write: Responses will vary.

Week 13 (pages 41–43)
MONDAY
1. declarative
2. "Why are you digging holes in your back yard, George?" asked his neighbor.

3. theme
4. daze—days: units of measurement equal to 24 hours; weak—week: unit of time measuring 7 days; knot—not: a negation; flours—flowers: blossoms
5. Answers will vary.

TUESDAY
1. terrain, disguise
2. looked
3. same root meaning life
4. Cross out not and in my opinion.
5. about 50 feet

WEDNESDAY
1. b, c
2. Answers will vary; to amuse
3. upbraid—rebuke; brusque—abrupt
4. foreign, height, deceive, shriek
5. 4, 1, 5, 3, 2

THURSDAY
1. land, landscape, lantern, laryngitis, lawless, lawn
2. Hardly anyone has squirrels in the backyard. No chipmunks live there either.
3. yes
4. squirrel, Greek, bushy, rodents, gnawing
5. Answers will vary. Possibilities:
   a. While I was eating my lunch, a squirrel hopped up on the railing and chattered at me.
   b. After the barbeque, we were surprised by the squirrels.
   c. A storm came up suddenly while I was mowing the lawn.
   d. When I came out the back door, I saw a chipmunk eating something out of the girl's orange backpack.

FRIDAY
Read: Answers will vary.
Write: Character sketches will vary.

Week 14 (pages 44–46)
MONDAY
1. imagery
2. tortillas, sundaes, soufflés, cheese or cheeses
3. c
4. A person who loves to eat is looking for a cook.
5. Answers will vary; preposterous – ordinary or simple; gigantic – tiny; extravagant – moderate; fetid – mild; superfluous – conservative; colossal – small

TUESDAY
1. ; (semicolon)
2. move away from
3. common: 5; proper: 3
4. no
5. Answers will vary; Three people hold records for eating surprising numbers of doughnuts in a short amount of time.

ANSWER KEY

WEDNESDAY
1. payable; prayed, carrying, fanciful
2. noun clause
3. expository
4. bad-smelling
5. Check to see that drawings fit with directions.

THURSDAY
1. thesaurus
2. It's a good idea to limit the children's intake of doughnuts in the morning, isn't it?
3. investigating
4. gerund phrase: Eating pizza; prepositional phrases: over 75 acres, of pizza, in a day
5. Answers will vary.

FRIDAY
1. three
2. $17.00
3. Answers will vary.
Write: Descriptive phrases will vary.

Week 15 (pages 47–49)
MONDAY
1. a. clown's tricks; b. clown's trick; c. clowns' trick; d. clowns' tricks
2. When the lion tamer hollered, "Look out!" Sam was so startled that he dropped his fire sticks.
3. The lion tamer hollering "Look Out!"
4. imminent
5. e, g, h

TUESDAY
1. manageable, difference, outrageous, immediately
2. A circus train has several kinds of cars
3. rich, excessive, splendid, expensive foods or furnishings or decorations
4. today's weather in Africa
5. Answers will vary.

WEDNESDAY
1. a. pre – before
   b. fore – in front of
   c. contra – against
2. Thai Elephant Orchestra, Lampang, Thailand, Founders, Asian
3. most noisy or noisiest
4. someone who is sick
5. Answers will vary; Circus-goers in London saw a unicyclist perform amazing juggling tricks while riding the unicycle.

THURSDAY
1. Drop *there*; In the second sentence, change *of* to *have*.
2. glossary
3. brutal, candle, classical
4. collar – to catch or crab
5. The Ringling Brothers-Barnum & Bailey Circus depends on its circus trains to move performers, animals, and equipment. The circus travels about 16,000 miles each year, and moving the circus is a major ordeal. Each train has a trainmaster whose job it is to keep the trains running well and operating on schedule. The trains can be 50–60 cars long. There are cars for performers, staff, maintenance crews, technicians, and animals. After the train reaches its destination, it takes 16 hours to unload the trains and set up for the shows.

FRIDAY
1. 79 years
2. 123 years
3. 1885
4. Answers will vary depending on year. In 2006—106 years
5. Jumbo and Gargantua
Write: Letters will vary.

Week 16 (pages 50–52)
MONDAY
1. resolution
2. you
3. Dear Dr. Drill: Yours truly,
4. Answers will vary. Synonyms: difficult, burdensome, hard; Antonyms: easy, leisurely
5. The gym will start to charge a fee for use of towels.

TUESDAY
1. no
2. strangely = adverb; human = adjective; is = verb
3. b
4. tornado, echo, alto
5. Answers will vary. The topic sentence should be something to this effect: Someone has set a new record for the heaviest weight lifted with an ear.

WEDNESDAY
1. On September 30, 2001, a team of body builders in Kenosha, Wisconsin pulled a 36,320-pound truck over three miles, setting a world record.
2. yes—look and are
3. The pushups are not very impressive or are worth little.
4. persuasive writing
5. 3, 4, 1, 5, 2

THURSDAY
1. loan, minor, navel, pact, taut, sighed
2. yes
3. in the 900s
4. hide, choose, lie, ring, throw, rise
5. Some people, such as Fuatai Solo, climb coconut trees for fun. When he broke the tree climbing record in Sukuna Park, Fiji Fuatai was so excited that he climbed the tree a second time. This time, as he climbed, he held the prize money in his teeth

FRIDAY
1. City Gym
2. Answers will vary; Susie Fisher probably tripped on her untied shoelace.
3. 29 seconds before the end of the race
4. A mouse walked across the chin-up bar.
5. 10 kilometers
6. Answers will vary. Both situations involved an interruption or incident that kept the athlete in first place from winning.
Write: Captions will vary.

Week 17 (pages 53–55)
MONDAY
1. The smallest muscle's length is five hundredths of an inch long.
2. run-on
3. yes
4. 15
5. b, d, e, f

TUESDAY
1. who, whom, what, whoever
2. Answers will vary; Al's leg bone cracked when he fell from the ladder.
3. gaff – gambit
4. should've; they're; won't; it'd
5. a. walk   d. ball
   b. down   e. nose
   c. head   f. house

WEDNESDAY
1. How I endured 970 Surgeries and Lived to Tell About Them
2. Answers will vary; The person had a lot of surgeries, and has a sense of humor.
3. amiable
4. A doctor measuring sneezes
5. aabbbb

THURSDAY
1. Change says to say.
2. At age 111, James Henry Brett, Jr. had a successful hip transplant, making him the oldest person on record to endure a surgery. This took place on November 7, 1960.
3. physicist
4. Answers will vary: immune system, immunity, or human body
5. Answers will vary.

FRIDAY
1. personification
2. – 4. Answers will vary.
Write: Revisions will vary. Misspelled words are: headache, molar, earache, enough, presidents, professional, athletes, aspirin, know

Week 18 (pages 56–58)
MONDAY
1. Isn't the largest shopping mall in the world the one in Edmonton, Alberta, Canada?
2. hyperbole
3. natural tendency
4. mice, oxen, antelopes, studios, chiefs, fathers-in-law
5. diamonds

TUESDAY
1. atlas
2. rhythm, answer, castle, laughter, llama, zipper
3. b
4. ic, al
5. PR, G, PA, G, I

WEDNESDAY
1. site
2. Whose
3. contagious, courteous, glamorous, malicious, genius, anonymous
4. onomatopoeia or sensory appeal, or repetition
5. a. O   c. F   e. O
   b. F   d. O

THURSDAY
1. Garth's Gold Specialties Company made a gold mousetrap for Dr. Rodenz's wife.
2. acrimony-bitterness; veritable-true; timorous-shy
3. Exhausted
4. Who would pay $350 for a yo-yo? In 1998, thousands of people paid this much for the Gold Fusion Yo-yo. It won the Coveted Toy Craze of the Year Award.
5. no

FRIDAY
Read: Answers may vary somewhat.
  Point of view 1: third person; 2: first person;
  Theme 1: shopping with little brother;
  2: shopping with little brother;
  Mood 1: playful, funny; 2: negative;
  Techniques used 1: narrative, active visual appeal, description, humor;
  2: warnings, persuasive writing, figurative language, repetition
Write: Summaries and titles will vary.

Week 19 (pages 59–61)
MONDAY
1. even though
2. championship
3. a
4. well-groomed, all-knowing, U-turn, forget-me-not
5. Only four countries have won the Water Polo World Championship twice.

TUESDAY
1. no
2. eventually, negligence, hopeless
3. minute, minute
4. swallow, swam, swatch, sweetheart, swimmer, sword
5. two

WEDNESDAY
1. rescue (or guard)
2. transitive: gave, wore; intransitive: did
3. no
4. After practicing for their ocean swim competition, Joe asked Max, "Have you ever heard a whale wail?"
5. Answers will vary.

THURSDAY
1. chided, scolded, criticized
2. lieutenant, deceived, counterfeit
3. winner of the 1978 World Championships
4. The farthest distance anyone has swum at one time is 2,360 miles.
5. no

FRIDAY
1. 6
2. 14 hr, 10 min
3. 1923–1927
4. about 25 years
5. August and September are the best months for an English Channel swim.
6. The swim must be easier going from France to England than from England to France
7. Answers will vary; discouraged.
Write: Comments and suggestions will vary.

Week 20 (pages 62–64)
MONDAY
1. We ate appetizers, salads, and pasta; then fish, rice, and vegetables; and finally, cake, pie, and ice cream.
2. b
3. yes
4. c
5. Predictions will vary.

TUESDAY
1. no
2. celebration or party
3. fraud, eloquent, beard, leopard
4. Cuban dancers thrilled the spectators at the world's largest dance festival. Over 4000 dancers entertained for ten days at the festival in Canta Catarina, Brazil.
5. party

WEDNESDAY
1. My favorite days of the year are the Fourth of July, Halloween, Valentine's Day, any Saturday, and any day in July.
2. confident
3. nominative
4. Just be tough and eat the garlic.
5. Amy's pet snail lost the race.

THURSDAY
1. complimented
2. radios, donkeys, buzzes, charities
3. still in her pajamas
4. Endings will vary.
5. The Chef refused to cook frog legs at a frog leg festival.

FRIDAY
1. power
2. 15 days
3. honored, esteemed, respected
4. The passage refers to the dragons as mythical.
5. The proverb means that someone hopes the child will grow up to be powerful and respected, as the dragon is.
Write: Student instructions will vary.

Week 21 (pages 65–67)
MONDAY
1. life
2. a
3. absence, sequence
4. narrative (or descriptive)
5. Responses will vary.

TUESDAY
1. no
2. gentle, tame
3. Popeye, the oldest snake on record, died in Philadelphia, Pennsylvania, on April 15, 1977 at the age of 40 years, 3 months, and 14 days.
4. goose, gore, gorgeous, gorilla, gosling, governor
5. Written experiences will vary.

WEDNESDAY
1. quarrel, quirky, quotient
2. logical
3. reflexive
4. a, c, d
5. evaluations will vary.

THURSDAY
1. nonfiction
2. The lion ran straight for the poodle.
3. What does the parrot think about the expression, "a bird's eye view"?
4. obstacles
5. Details will vary.

FRIDAY
Read: Watch to see how well students follow the written directions.
Write: Poems will vary.

Week 22 (pages 68–70)
MONDAY
1. auto = self; mid = middle; cir = circle; uni = one
2. Joe's; journeys' ends
3. has dreaded
4. Poet does not believe St. Brendan's tales are true.
5. Comparisons will vary. Both address the same story. The two have different biases or conclusions about the truth of St. Brendan's claims.

TUESDAY
1. FBI, Civil War, Middle Ages, Kleenex
2. through
3. Answers will vary.
   The connotation of *criticize* is a situation in which someone is put on the spot while someone else finds fault with him or her or with an accomplishment, performance, or behavior.
   Ridicule has the added connotation of being made fun of, laughed at, or shamed.
4. 1122

5. Two brothers from the USA hold a record for the longest team motorcycle ride. Chris and Erin Ratay rode 101,322 miles through the continents of Asia, Africa, North America, South America, Europe, and Australia. They left Morocco on May 21, 1999 and ended their trip in New York City on August 6, 2003.

WEDNESDAY
1. Drop at.
2. outrageous
3. traveling across the country on a skateboard
4. abab
5. Summaries will vary. People can set records for journeys by traveling long periods of time in unusual vehicles.

THURSDAY
1. wily, lucky
2. doleful–cheerful; truncate–extend
3. the bathtub sailors were safe on the shore
4. title page
5. herculean

FRIDAY
1. 5, 1, 6, 4, 7, 3, 8, 2
2. She must be bold and adventuresome.
3. 101
4. – 5. Answers will vary.
Write: Arguments will vary.

Week 23 (pages 71–73)
MONDAY
1. Answers will vary; blastoff, offset, sendoff, takeoff, runoff, castoff, cutoff, takeoff, handoff, offset, off-season, offstage, offshore, offspring, offline, offhand, offbeat,
2. knickers, scheme, write, pseudonym
3. tourist, trip, rocket, trip, dollars
4. things that burn up in space and look like shooting stars
5. Most of the streaking, burning lights in space are not stars. Instead they are meteors or comets.

TUESDAY
1. nonessential
2. seemingly true but somehow suspicious
3. Topic sentences will vary.
4. After the space trip (which, by the way departed by accident) the space tourist had a long spell of dizziness.
5. Nothing can escape because the force of gravity of a black hole is so strong.

WEDNESDAY
1. waxing
2. whom, ourselves, yours
3. enough, people
4. imagery
5. Answers will vary. The people of long ago did not understand natural phenomena to the extent we do today. They believed in gods that controlled natural happenings

and used them to reward or punish people on earth.

THURSDAY
1. new, a fiction book
2. Scarcely anybody isn't impressed by the launch of a rocket.
3. thesaurus
4. Answers will vary. Students should replace *saw, yelled, went,* and perhaps *launch.*
5. Sue Spacey
1313 Corral Rd.
Keno, OR 97591
NASA Headquarters
Suite IM32
Washington, D.C. 20546
To Whom It May Concern:
I am looking for information about comets. Can you send me anything?
Yours truly,
Sue Spacey

FRIDAY
1. 41 years
2. 1946
3. 1961
4. dogs
5. fish, spiders
Write: Beginnings, endings, and titles will vary.

Week 24 (pages 74–76)
MONDAY
1. Underneath the picnic blanket the ground is thick with bugs, rocks, worms, and sand.
2. basketfuls, families, banjos
3. tardy
4. c
5. Answers will vary.

TUESDAY
1. yesterday, greedily, seldom, so, so, fast
2. ogres, practiced, bizarre, etiquette, kazoos
3. irregular, extraterrestrial, supersonic, monotone
4. biography
5. Answers will vary. Check for active verbs.

WEDNESDAY
1. rhyme, rhythm, onomatopoeia
2. bold
3. "What to Do After Eating the World's Largest Watermelon"
4. Drop "they."
5. Check drawings to see that students have followed directions correctly.

THURSDAY
1. I told Abby a story, and she believed it all.
2. realized, promised, surprise, apologize
3. A. a watermelon's seeds;
B. two picnic baskets' handles;
C. the onions' smell
4. Cross out: it, is a stomach, is a stomach
5. Descriptions will vary.

FRIDAY
1. Sprinkle with cheese.
2. smoothness, creamy, ooze, trickle

3. brown sugar and barbecue sauce
4. a hovering cloud
5. Answers will vary.
Write: Recipes and descriptions will vary.

Week 25 (pages 77–79)
MONDAY
1. They all have a silent letter.
2. largest = adjective;
in = preposition;
down = adverb;
speeds = noun
3. twelfth, license, remedy, trouble
4. personification
5. a. hundred year-old trees were snapped like twigs.
b. The eruption was triggered;
c. Fifty-seven people died;
d. Mudslides destroyed the foliage

TUESDAY
1. deadliest
2. title, author's last name, publisher (in a library, call number)
3. A group of Spanish tourists, led by Guide Laroux, visited Mt. St. Helens after the eruption.
4. overwhelmed, flooded
5. Answers will vary.

WEDNESDAY
1. yes
2. childish, ashen, golden
3. mischievous, foreign, reign
4. Predictions will vary.
5. poetry

THURSDAY
1. Outback Steakhouse,
Pvt. James Cohen,
Nashville Chamber of Commerce
(Other phrases are correct as is.)
2. dissent, hire, currant
3. gerund
4. The mountain's eruption created an 80,000-foot ash cloud in 15 minutes. Some ash circled the Earth.
5. 1,314 feet

FRIDAY
1. hard to catch or find
2. high in the Himalayan Mountains
3. long-haired creature, tall, upright, primate-like, ape-like
4. Author leans toward the belief that the yeti could exist.
5. Answers will vary. Check to make sure the circled sentences are correctly identified as fact or opinion.
Write: Personal responses and pictures will vary.

Week 26 (pages 80–82)
MONDAY
1. a. Who's;
b. who's;
c. whomever;
d. Who

2. a restaurant in Saratoga Springs, New York
3. An inventor is someone who thinks up and creates new ideas and items. An itinerant is someone who wanders.
4. My favorite inventions are these: the zipper, marshmallows, electric toothbrushes, and trains.
5. Summaries will vary.

TUESDAY
1. omitted, embarrass, horrid, memory, staccato, parallel
2. Popsicles, sandwiches, and potato chips
3. yes
4. Popsicle
5. Answers will vary. It is said that the Popsicle was invented by accident. Eleven-year old Frank Epperson was trying to make his own soda pop. He mixed soda powder and water in a bucket. The mixture was left outside with the wooden stirring stick standing in the liquid. The next morning the liquid was frozen. Frank picked it up by the stick, tasted it, and loved it. He began to sell "Epperson Icicles" for a nickel. Eventually, he changed the name of the treat to "Popsicles."

WEDNESDAY
1. illicit: unlawful; elicit: to call forth
2. "Is it true," asked Jason, "that the waffle was invented when someone wearing a metal suit sat on a pancake?"
3. descriptive
4. He is discovering. We discover.
5. Impressions will vary.

THURSDAY
1. Replacements will vary.
2. Sentences will vary.
3. restaurant, people, interesting, friend
4. the history or derivation
5. a, d, e

FRIDAY
1. falling apple, kite, atom, x-rays, medical discovery, air travel
2. x-rays, falling apple (gravity)
3. gravity
4. Answers will vary; something to do with flying or flight
5. Answers will vary; antibiotics
Write: Headlines will vary.

Week 27 (pages 83–85)
MONDAY
1. The world's largest Popsicle contained enough liquid to make 250,000 ice cubes and weighed 17,450 pounds.
2. Answers will vary. (overtime, override, overall, rollover, sleepover, stopover, layover)
3. pizzas, foxes, geese, jealousies, vetoes, wives, children, trousers
4. mood
5. A. missing pizza;
   B. 1 year and 1 day

TUESDAY
1. The prize-winner looked respectable, but he had some secrets that may make him seem less respectable.
2. Joe took one look at the world's largest donut and yelled, "I want a bite!"
3. To measure the largest dog biscuit
4. no
5. Eliminate biggest, in Pasadena, California, in weight, and diameter.

WEDNESDAY
1. ed = eat; rot = turn; dorm = sleep
2. gentleman, coconut, circumference, weighed
3. no
4. a. touch; b. smell, c. taste
5. a – c: Comparisons will vary; d. c

THURSDAY
1. wondered: past; would break: future; wonders: present
2. Alfred J. Cobb, grower of the heaviest cucumber, won an award in September, 2003.
3. a quotation index
4. mania
5. Topic sentences will vary.

FRIDAY
1. The world's largest banana split is on display.
2. People that could visit the banana split.
3. To encourage people to visit the banana split exhibit.
4. proudly wearing puffy hats of sweet marshmallow cream
5. 1,300
Write: Descriptive words and phrases will vary.

Week 28 (pages 86–88)
MONDAY
1. Answers will vary. sandstorm, thunderstorm, windstorm
2. The, Boston, Celtics, National, Basketball, League
3. player, L.A. Laker
4. persuasive writing
5. Answers will vary. There are different ways that these lines can form a sensible poem. One possibility for the numbering from top to bottom is 3, 8, 2, 6, 1, 5, 7, 4

TUESDAY
1. required
2. lovable, sensible
3. Answers will vary.
4. Answers will vary.
5. drama: 511; dowse: not on any page here, probably on page 509; dribble: 513; dread: 512

WEDNESDAY
1. A Romanian-born basketball player, who is 91 inches tall, is the tallest man to play in the National Basketball League.
2. direct objects: cheers, pyramid, pompons

3.   sullen: gloomy; pretense: an insincere show
4. Answers will vary.
5. Inferences will vary.

THURSDAY
1. mystified, envied, paid, defied, worried, played
2. heel, heal
3. fiction
4. Answers will vary.
5. strange: adjective; High: adjective; very: adverb; disappeared: verb; under: preposition; hurriedly: adverb; room: noun; none: pronoun (or predicate pronoun)

FRIDAY
1. 4,600 square feet
2. Answers will vary: (e.g: four 3-point field goals)
3. Inferences will vary: (e.g: The player fouled out or got kicked out of the game, or the player was not put into the game to play, or the player did a bad job and got taken out.)
4. to inform a reader about basketball; someone who is interested in learning about the game or does not know much about basketball
5. when the player has fouled the maximum number of times allowed (5 or 6)
Write: Lists of rhyming words and poems will vary.

Week 29 (pages 89–91)
MONDAY
1. ricotta
2. around, for, in
3. anniversary, anonymous, Antarctica, architect
4. stereotype
5. Conclusions will vary.

TUESDAY
1. genuine
2. Shania, Twain, Queen, Country, Music, Come, Over (Sometimes every word in a title is capitalized so On is also an acceptable answer.)
3. to buy
4. to inform readers about the world's fastest rapper
5. Written raps will vary.

WEDNESDAY
1. evoke
2. effect
3. Misplaced modifier: in the garbage can. Rewrites of the sentence will vary. By mistake, Joe dropped into the garbage can the music he had written.
4. Someone thought an important person had moved out of his or her home, until the person assumed gone showed up at the door.
5. a–b–c–b–d–b–e–b–b

ANSWER KEY

THURSDAY
1. Legend, a music album by Jamaican Bob Marley, is the best-selling reggae album of all time.
2. denotation
3. a. b
4. Errors fixed: Lennon's 1965 Rolls Royce, $229,900; guitar; Jerry Garcia's electric guitar; Elvis Presley's guitar, $180,000; Charlie Parker's saxophone,; Buddy Holly's electric guitar, $110,000
5. yes

FRIDAY
1. people attending the rock concert
2. to inform concert-goers about the concert
3. two
4. probably not
5. Responses will vary.
Write: Designs and biographies will vary.

Week 30 (pages 92–94)
MONDAY
1. dumbstruck, scene, ledge, chasm, gnarled, wedged, bridge
2. The weather service gave the tornado warning too soon.
3. compound-complex
4. first person
5. The strength of the winds in the tornado picked them up, and they got caught up in the trees.

TUESDAY
1. C (Colombian); M and N (mother nature); R (renaissance); S, F, F (sir frances frieze)
2. 3 (fastest, solar, 1,500)
3. skillful
4. torment, torpedo, torrid, torque
5. Rewrites will vary.

WEDNESDAY
1. infinitesimal, miniscule
2. that I have seen in this area so far; adjective
3. frivolous, musician, ingenious
4. c, d
5. The first two sentences are facts; the last two are opinions.

THURSDAY
1. I know of no area that gets more snowfall than Mt. Rainier, Washington.
2. A. interaction; B. atypical; C. equilateral
3. The greatest depth of snow measured was found at Tamarac, California, USA. The measurement was taken in March, 1911.
4. Paraphrases will vary somewhat. Be prepared for a tornado by storing supplies in the lowest part of your building. In the event of a tornado, take shelter indoors in a low area, away from doors and windows. If you are caught outside, try to stay out of cars and take shelter by staying in a ditch or under a bridge.
5. under a bridge or in a ditch

FRIDAY
1. b

2. wetter
3. Darwin and Cairns
4. The northern part gets more rain than the southern part.
5. Areas with stripes receive over 20 inches of rainfall a year
Write: Weather report hyperbole statements will vary.

Week 31 (pages 95–97)
MONDAY
1. fourth, forth
2. no
3. tone
4. lie: present participle – is lying; past – lay; past participle – has lain
   lay: present participle – is laying; past – laid; past participle – has laid
5. Check to see that directions are followed correctly.

TUESDAY
1. refute
2. The editor, on the other hand, argued in favor of the plan for a new bridge.
3. objective
4. Anne does all the puzzles in the paper every day. When she finishes the pun cipher, she starts on the first crossword puzzle. After finishing both crossword puzzles, Anne decides to try the tongue twister.
5. No, you cannot be sure, because there may be more than one of a puzzle on a page.

WEDNESDAY
1. radical, spiral, model
2. a. one puzzle's clues;
   b. two puzzles' clues;
   c. one wife's paper;
   d. the wives' papers
3. American – belonging to; earthen – made of; lifelike – resembling
4. irony
5. Headlines will vary.

THURSDAY
1. talkative
2. yes
3. under a pseudonym
4. the Internet or a quotation index
5. d

FRIDAY
Read:
1. The puzzle is finished, and the clues are blank.
2. newspapers
3. cash, reads, classified, stop, report
4. cash, report
5. Answers will vary. (could be stop, circulation, paper, report, cash)
Write: Clues will vary somewhat, but should give a clear enough definition so that another person could solve the puzzle.

Week 32 (pages 98–100)
MONDAY
1. exemplary, exciting, exquisite, extremely, exceptional, exotic
2. aggravated
3. a. Since we were running out of air;
   b. that we get back to the surface quickly;
   c. because we started our ascent in time to avoid danger
4. Answers may vary. The author seems to disapprove of the idea of wheelbarrow racing.
5. People race long distances pushing wheelbarrows.

TUESDAY
1. Answers will vary: fight
2. yes
3. exclamation point
4. all but the last one: weather forecasts
5. Revisions will vary.

WEDNESDAY
1. "Let's race our camel at the Geelong Camel Cup Carnival," Sam suggested to Sara. "We could win a thousand dollars."
2. splendid
3. Oh, no!
4. Replacements will vary. Students should replace *carry* and *run*.
5. a. egg – cracked;
   b. shoe-in – boot;
   c. cow-riding – moo-ving;
   d. dough – penny
   e. potato – eyes, appealing

THURSDAY
1. contest: protest or argue against; contest: competition
2. infinitive phrase
3. reigning, deceitful, conceited, neighbor
4. glossary
5. Revisions will vary.

FRIDAY
Read:
1. expository
2. In the last sentence, the author infers that many people are comfortable with bugs.
3. About 14 feet
4. Answers will vary.
5. The cricket spitter must be careful not to swallow the cricket.
Write: Explanations will vary.

Week 33 (pages 101–103)
MONDAY
1. ellipsis
2. resolution
3. Answers will vary. Connotation might include singing around a fire, camping trips, kids' camps, roasting marshmallows, telling ghost stories
4. cause: not breaking in the new boots; effect: George got blisters.
5. a. IN   d. E
   b. D   e. E
   c. IM   f. IM

TUESDAY
1. brought, chocolate, mosquito, repellent, license
2. form = shape
3. Drop they, totally and, they just saw
4. a biographical dictionary
5. interrogative: whose, which
   possessive: mine, yours
   intensive: myself
   demonstrative: that, this, it
   indefinite: it, everybody
   reflexive: myself

WEDNESDAY
1. Who was it that asked, "Do you hear a bear breathing heavily outside this ten?t"
2. dry firewood
3. A. peek, peak; B. bear, bare
4. sign about coyotes
5. Summaries will vary; the animals cause problems, so watch out for them.

THURSDAY
1. rascal (All others are verbs.)
2. Change each "of" to "have."
3. parenthetical, simultaneously
4. no
5. Rewrites will vary.

FRIDAY
Read:
1. # 1
2. wind's strong arms, wind shook the tent with angry claws
3. Answers will vary.
4. a dark night with the tent whipping in the wind and frightened, pale campers shaking inside the tent huddled around a faint, fading flashlight
5. hearing, sight
Write: Story endings will vary.

Week 34 (pages 104–106)
MONDAY
1. a colon
2. survive: verb; without: pronoun; higher: adjective
3. a fake
4. onomatopoeia
5. This allowed Steven to have water to drink. Without water, he would not have survived.

TUESDAY
1. fight
2. lose
3. transitive
4. nibbled
5. 22 or 23, depending on whether it was a Leap Year

WEDNESDAY
1. head
2. monkeying, monkied; worrying, worried; muddying, muddied
3. a and c
4. simile
5. a. She was rescued;
   b. The skier got lost;
   c. Steven was able to drink pure water;

d. the elevator car fell 75 stories;
e. Bev was stuck in the store overnight

THURSDAY
1. Former, Olympic, Eric Lemarque, California's, Sierra, Nevada, Mountains
2. succumb, perish
3. On July 28, 1945, Bethany Lou Oliver survived a 1,000-foot fall in an elevator at the Empire State Building in New York City, New York.
4. surreptitious, surrender, surplice, surplus, survival, survive
5. a. well to good; b. surely to sure;
   c. quick to quickly; d. real to really;
   e. lay to lie; f. risen to raised;
   g. bad to badly

FRIDAY
Read:
1. amazing survivals
2. 1988 Kively Popa John – "Fortunately she had just been to the market . . ."
3. Answers will vary, as there are several facts.
4. the surgeries
5. Answers will vary.
Write: Titles and questions will vary.

Week 35 (pages 107–109)
MONDAY
1. The Last Baseball Game by Claus D. Park
2. skidded about half the distance between the two bases
3. discouraging
4. metaphor
5. One possible sequence numbering:
   8, 5, 3, 1, 7, 2, 4, 6

TUESDAY
1. "How come" should be "Why."
2. There are none.
3. Answers will vary; anger or rage
4. baseball
5. Revisions will vary.

WEDNESDAY
1. contagious
2. You've got to remember that it's only Tom's first time at bat in his whole life.
3. imagery
4. a. screaming = gerund;
   b. screaming = participle;
   c. to scream = infinitive;
   d. screaming = participle
5. Music at baseball games used to be provided by live organists, but this has been replaced by recorded music.

THURSDAY
1. mistake
2. baseball, shot
3. no
4. thesaurus, cougar, anguish, beard, drought, boisterous
5. Captions will vary.

FRIDAY
1. first person

2. The author hit a baseball that broke someone's window. He (She) is apologizing.
3. Answers will vary.
4. Answers will vary.
Write: Poems will vary.

Week 36 (pages 110–112)
MONDAY
1. nuisance, consequence
2. scarcity, shortage
3. a. action; b. action; c. linking
4. personification
5. Inferences will vary.

TUESDAY
1. unhealthy
2. yes
3. I learned from an almanac that the population of Sao Paulo, Brazil increases by 2,000 people a day.
4. Answers will vary.
5. Middletown, Connecticut is a small city of 45,000 people situated in a pleasant spot along the Connecticut River. In recent years, the city is growing and becoming a particularly attractive setting for new businesses. Thirty-five businesses have opened in a downtown mall called the Main Street Market. Other additions are two new golf courses and a new 12-screen movie theater complex.

WEDNESDAY
1. Todd and his friend were very happy.
2. h – honest; h – ghost;
   p – psychic; k – knight;
   g – gnome; t – gourmet;
   w – wrestler
3. no
4. true
5. Answers will vary. Fairview and Midway are 1 and 2 on both lists. Riverside, Franklin, and Oak Grove are on both lists. Four names show up on each list that are not on the other list.

THURSDAY
1. lunar = moon;
   mortal = death;
   dissect = cut;
   portable = carry;
   dynamite = power;
   dormant = sleep
2. Venice, a city in Italy, has the distinction of being the world's most waterlogged city. OR Venice (a city in Italy) has the distinction of being the world's most waterlogged city.
3. index
4. no
5. Eliminate a city in England, top of the chart, in the population

FRIDAY
1. – 2. Answers will vary.
Write: Answers will vary.

Use It! Don't Lose It! IP 612-3